Holiday Road

Holiday Road
A Memoir

SHELLEY COSTELLO

Copyright © 2011 by Shelley Costello.

Library of Congress Control Number:		2011903095
ISBN:	Hardcover	978-1-4568-7399-8
	Softcover	978-1-4568-7398-1
	Ebook	978-1-4568-7400-1

All rights reserved. No part of this book may be reproduced or transmitted in any form or by any means, electronic or mechanical, including photocopying, recording, or by any information storage and retrieval system, without permission in writing from the copyright owner.

For various reasons I've decided to change the names of everyone in this book. All the place names remain as they are, and any facts and figures mentioned in this book are as I understand them to be.

This book was printed in the United States of America.

To order additional copies of this book, contact:
Xlibris Corporation
0-800-644-6988
www.xlibrispublishing.co.uk
Orders@xlibrispublishing.co.uk
301284

Contents

Grace 9
Welcome to California 14
Ashtanga Yoga 24
Good News and Bad News 38
Cool 45
Garage Yoga 52
Fourth of July Weekend 58
Oyster Mushrooms, Ashtanga, and Tarzan 69
Morning Campers! 81
A Concrete Ship, Castroville, and Monterey Beach 94
Laguna Seca Mazda Raceway Grand Prix Campsite 101
Big Sur and McWay Falls 113
Plaskett Creek and Sand Dollar Beach 119
Morro Rock and Gaviota Beach 132
Fifteenth of July 141
Disneyland and Vanessa's Tenth Birthday 145
Sequoia National Park 155
Another Practice 162
Lake Tahoe 173
Birthdays Barbeque 183
Lake Tahoe Revisited 188
San Francisco Zoo 195
One More Class 207
Long Way Down the Holiday Road 212

For my brother Rich

Grace

I've been planning our trip to California for almost a year. It's been six whole years since I visited during the summer months, and I am excited about having two whole months to enjoy spending time with my brother Tom and his family.

How part of my family ended up living in California is down to my sister, Kate, who met someone in the U.S. Air Force and moved there when she was just sixteen. She got Dad's permission to get married (in the end) and move to California, had two beautiful boys, who are now twenty-one and twenty-two, got divorced, and became a successful real estate agent. She married again, and after a second divorce, she met Antonio, who lives in San Francisco and whom she has now been with for about a year. They hope to move in together sometime next year.

My brother Tom visited her when he was eighteen and, during his stay, fell in love with her best friend's sister, Shelby. They were married soon after that, and Tom has lived there ever since. They have one child, Sam, who is twelve.

Kate became an American citizen long ago and petitioned for our parents to live over there. They emigrated two years ago, and rather than enjoying retirement, they now spend most of their time working, oh, and frequenting far too many casinos!

Up until four years ago, my life was pretty chaotic: moving from one bad relationship to another, and despite having a pretty successful career, I've always felt unfulfilled. Two failed marriages and two beautiful children later, I decided enough was enough and took stock of my life, became single, requalified myself, and became self-employed, working as a yoga teacher and life coach. This gives me lots of free time to tend to my children, Vanessa and Leon, and our home life, which, in itself, is a full-time job. Four years is a long time to be single, but during that time, I've been able to reconnect with my true self and discover my true passion in life: yoga.

I first discovered yoga shortly after my last relationship ended, when I joined a study group at the school where I started taking my coaching course. I mentioned to someone that I'd been reading about the natural laws of the universe and other self-improvement books, and they suggested I try yoga. Being the bookworm that I am, I bought a book and then soon realised that the only way to truly discover yoga is through practice. I joined a class soon after, took my teacher-qualification course, and have been practising ever since.

About a year ago, I started practising Ashtanga yoga, which is more physically demanding and consists of several series (levels). I practise the primary series four to six times a week, and my whole life really revolves around yoga in some way or another. For me, it isn't just about the physical practice but actually living as a yogi too. This comes easy because having lived such a chaotic and destructive life for most of my adulthood, I feel I have 'been there and done it and have enough T-shirts' to last me a lifetime. It isn't hard to make healthy choices; they just happen naturally—becoming a vegetarian, not drinking alcohol, eating a healthy, balanced diet, and surrounding myself with a lot of positive influences. I think I'm also doing my children a huge favour by introducing them to this way of thinking, and although I allow them to make their own choices, I know it's all being absorbed and will benefit them enormously as they grow up.

So, being my own boss, I've decided we'll take the whole summer out and spend it in California. I started saving shortly after the dismal summer we experienced a year ago. If you live in England, you'll understand what I am talking about—you know, summers with little sunshine and a bucket load of rain. Everything we planned last summer was rained off, and despite going ahead with most of our days out, and having a good time regardless, we've decided that we want sunshine guaranteed.

Tom suggested we go on a camping trip while we are there. He and Shelby are going to plan their summer vacation around us being there, and so he has become the master planner in mapping out our assault along the California coastal highway.

There have been many times in my life when I've made a decision that I want to live in California. I first visited when I was just sixteen. My dad sent me because he and my mum were in complete despair over my wild child behaviour. I dismally failed my exams and was shipped off to California for three whole months during the summer of 1989. My dad said this would get me away from bad influences, and he entrusted me in to the care of my older sister, Kate. I have to say, I could think of worse places to be shipped off to.

I fell in love with California that summer, as well as a boy called Zac, and returned the following summer for another three months. I fell in love with a marine called William that time, but those trips had sowed the seeds, and part of my heart has always been in California since then.

Hindsight is a beautiful thing. If I had half the sense that I have now, I would have applied to emigrate back then. If Kate had sponsored me, the whole process would have taken between five and seven years, making me still only in my early twenties. However, it wasn't meant to be, and there were so many other things that seemed far more exciting in my life that time just passed away. Shortly after the second summer in California, I met my first husband, and so, then began my twenty-year journey through the choppy waters of bad relationships and lots of destructive, chaotic behaviour to mix life up a little.

There was one time when I actually came very close to living there. I'd got back in touch with William (the marine I had met when I was seventeen) and left my first husband to fly over to California to meet him. Talk about whirlwind. It had been seven years since we'd seen each other, and he was in a completely different place than I was. He was a Christian and so, trying his best to do the 'right thing' (which wasn't easy where I was concerned). He proposed, and I flew back home to finalise everything in England, but a week before the wedding, I called it off, and that was the end of that. I jumped straight into another relationship and off I went again.

I visited California several more times and have visited with Vanessa a couple of times when she was younger. It felt the same, and I wanted to live there, but it just didn't seem like an option at the time and, of course, there was always some relationship going on in the background. The application process seemed to get more and more complicated, and for some reason, that now I just accept it obviously wasn't meant to be at the time, it didn't happen.

We last visited during Christmas 2007. One of my three other brothers and sister, who live in England (no, surprisingly we are not Catholic), came too, and we had a real family Christmas with our parents, Kate, Tom, and the rest of the family.

This summer visit, however, seems different somehow. I think, at some level of my being I hope I will meet the elusive 'Mr Right'. I've not wanted to meet anyone before this point because I've been immersed in too much self-improvement and studying for the past four years to have any time for a relationship.

Since the age of fourteen, I've never been without a boyfriend. As soon as one relationship ended, another would begin; sometimes, although I hate to admit this, the relationship hadn't even ended before I started a new one, but that's another story. Suffice to say, for twenty years one relationship merged into another, and they seemed to become more dysfunctional as time went on.

Four years being single, therefore, has really been a much-needed break, and although I feel like I am becoming somewhat of a tree-hugging (I do love trees) bhikkhuni (female Buddhist monk) and a devoted yogini, I've retained my fire and passion and feel I could probably now find some time in my life for someone else. I'm also pretty happy and functional these days, so maybe the next relationship will be a long-lasting one. Living in a bubble of being the princess in a fairytale, waiting for my knight galloping in on his white horse! Most definitely, because despite having all those failed relationships, all I ever really wanted was to fall in love and live happily ever after.

Everything I've intended for myself over the past couple of years has manifested itself in my life somehow, and I have a strong feeling that this summer is going to make that dream of 'happily ever after' come true.

Welcome to California

My stomach feels like it's jumping into my throat as the plane drops again, preparing to land. I look out of the window, see the bay below, and get that happy, tingly feeling in my stomach that only California seems to bring. The plane dips lower; my stomach flips again, and I can hear the noise of the landing gear engaging. It's difficult to tell how high we are from the water, but it seems far too close to me. We must be landing soon, because if we don't, I think we'll actually plunge into the water. I look down, wondering whether the white surf is actually big waves that look small because we are so high up or whether we are actually going to nosedive at any moment. I remind myself that I am not scared of flying any more, take a deep breath in, and drag my eyes away from the window. Vanessa and Leon still have their earphones on even though the radio and TV have been turned off. Vanessa is madly sucking sweets because she insists it stops her ears from popping, any excuse I say. Leon is bouncing his blue ted up and down on his knee. I look out of the window again and wince as I think perhaps I was right to be scared of flying. How close is that water!

We bumpily touch down, and Vanessa and Leon giggle as they jolt forward in their seats. It's just before 2.00 p.m. I silently thank God for not plunging me into the freezing cold bay water and breathe out.

The sun is now shining so brightly through the window that it's blinding. I am really going to welcome this warm weather. There is nothing like California sunshine. I know there's only one sun, but it's never the same back home. I wonder sometimes if it's the backdrop of the azure blue sky that does it. In England, the sun is never that bright and the sky never that blue.

'I'm so excited about seeing everyone,' Vanessa cries, clapping her hands.

'Me too!' Leon says excitedly, jumping up from his chair.

'Sit down, Leon, just until we stop,' I say, trying not to squash his excitement too much.

Leon is bouncy and reminds me of myself when I was younger. He has so much energy, and if that energy isn't being channelled somehow, well, then it was just bouncing around the walls or environment we happen to be in at the time. My yoga teacher said to me once that boys are generally like that, but as time goes on, and I have met some of his school friends, I've begun to see that Leon really does have a little more energy than most boys. Not a bad thing, just not great when you are confined to the space of, say, an aircraft!

Despite his boundless energy, and me being his mother and obviously very biased, Leon definitely lives up to the ideal of his blond hair and blue eyes: utterly adorable, charming, sweet-natured, and loving. He's very tall for his age and having Vanessa, who is four years older, I have to often remind myself he has only just turned six and still very much a little boy.

Our trip so far has gone perfectly: no delays and the flight has been a smooth one with no turbulence, which I am thankful for. Despite always having had a fear of flying, I have, over the past couple of years, managed to control this with some yogic breathing. The epiphany happened in 2006 over the Irish Sea, returning back to England after meeting my sister Kate in Ireland. I still drank back then and so, although my head was swimming in a shot of vodka to numb the flying fears, I spent most of the short flight with my head down, eyes closed, and gripping the seat so tightly, my knuckles were white. I was only there for a weekend and dreading, having to fly back home so soon. We had just taken off, and the panic quickly set in. I can't really say what happened, but I suddenly realised that I was being totally irrational and then felt an overwhelming sense of calm, and the fear of falling 30,000 feet into the sea left me. Saying that, I think there is still a little fear there somewhere, especially landing in San Francisco where you have to come in to land over the water, but I am, however, pleased not to have needed to put my yogic breathing to good use during the flight!

We're fortunate to be seated near to the front of the plane and, therefore, are some of the first to leave.

Our bags are already spinning around on the carousel as we head into the baggage claim area.

'There it is!' Leon exclaims, obviously having seen one of our cases, running towards the carousel.

'He'll never pull that off the carousel,' I say to Vanessa, speeding up a little to reach Leon before he attempts it.

'Well, he might, Mum, but he'll pull himself over with it,' she replies, giggling.

Vanessa is mature beyond her years. She is due to turn ten in a couple of weeks but often gives me advice and talks to me like she is the parent and I am the child. Like her brother, she is sweet-natured but very stubborn, and, with the sudden onset of a hormone rush, seems to be turning into a teenager far too many years before her time.

Quite the opposite of Leon, she has light brown hair and big green eyes, with eyelashes that put mine to shame. Her hair just reaches the small of her back, and I am immensely proud of the fact that she has such long, beautiful, curly hair.

When I was little, my hair was cut so short that I was often mistaken for a boy. In those days, the style was very much 'page boy', with a fringe; my hair just didn't grow right and so was probably better off, short. As I grew up, I resented this enormously and never seemed to be able to grow my hair. Fortunately, it now sits at my shoulders. When I had Vanessa, I made a silent commitment to myself never to cut her hair and so, apart from the odd trim here and there, have left Vanessa's hair to grow abundantly long.

We pick up our pace to catch Leon before he reaches the case.

We've travelled light, which is easier with it being summer, and in California, that means swimsuits, shorts, and flip-flops. We have so many pairs of flip flops that between the three of us we could open a flip-flop shop. When we packed a week ago, Vanessa counted them on the bed, announcing that there were twenty-seven pairs! I'm not quite sure how we managed to accumulate so many, but each time I went shopping, I somehow seemed to find another pair, and then I think I just forgot how many pairs I'd already bought.

Our cases are also packed full of goodies. Whenever anyone visits California from England, they always ask ahead of time what they need to bring, and our trip is no exception. Although you can buy British food in America, you can't buy everything, and because what you can buy is imported, it can be expensive. We have essentials such as brown sauce, salad cream, several pots of Bisto gravy granules, lemon curd, custard powder, chilli con carne mixes, Wispa bars, Curly Wurlys, chocolate Turkish Delights, Cadburys Dairy Milk and Fruit and Nut bars, Walkers crisps (they have to be): smokey bacon and beef and onion flavour, which I am sure are probably now the size of hundreds and thousands, red laces (to eat, not for your shoes), and half a dozen large cherry bakewells.

Kate is meeting us at the airport with Antonio, who we haven't met before.

Kate is five years older than me, smart, funny, and with a heart as big as her boobs . . . which are real, I have to say, feeling green with envy. Kate and I have different mothers, but she was also raised by my mother and, as with all my brothers and sisters, we make no differentiation between one another just because some of us have different mothers than others. She did, however, obviously inherit her mother's assets. Shame we couldn't just choose those genes . . . anyway, moving on.

Despite being quite petite at five foot three, Kate is as strong as an ox and a complete gym fiend. She can be found each morning at 6.00 a.m., pounding the treadmill and taking a highly energetic TRX class. She's highly competitive, which in real estate is a perfect attribute, and loves nothing more than a family night filled with wine and games, which she will fight to the death to win, and you have to play by the rules or else! Kate also inherited her mother's long, straight hair, which she has coloured blonde and tumbles loosely around her shoulders. She typifies real estate and fits perfectly into the glamorous lifestyle that comes with it.

Kate, like me, has been married and divorced twice (yes, I know it is rather coincidental, but we won't go there) and I admire her for having not settled for anything less than happiness. She met Antonio while on a girls' night out in San Francisco. They had spent all night engrossed in conversation; he'd walked her home and slept on the couch, and they have pretty much been together ever since.

Some people meet, fall in love, and have babies; and some meet, fall in love, and have a dog. Kate and Antonio decided on the latter. Henry is a Yorkshire terrier, and from the photos we have seen, he looks adorable.

Vanessa loves dogs and, in fact, I would go so far as to say that she loves dogs more than she does people. Ever since being old enough to talk, she has wanted one. My dad had a dog when Vanessa was born, and she used to cuddle and talk to her as soon as she could walk. She was even present at the birth of her litter of puppies, and so looking back, I think that experience made a firm impression on little Vanessa and is the foundation from which her love for dogs grew. Although I don't dislike dogs, I don't share her passion and can't quite bring myself to take on the responsibility of owning one.

Vanessa can't wait to meet Henry, and I actually think she is more excited about meeting Henry than anyone else.

'I am so excited about seeing Henry!' Vanessa says as we make our way through customs. 'Do you think I'll be able to hold his lead, Mum?'

'I'm sure you will,' I say, knowing that she won't take no for an answer, anyway.

We walk into the arrival area and spot Kate. It's hard not to spot her, with two enormous helium balloons and flowers.

She runs towards us. 'Welcome to California!' she says excitedly, handing me the flowers and Vanessa and Leon, a balloon each.

Henry is as expected, adorable, and it's immediately apparent that he, Vanessa, and Leon are going to become inseparable. He wags his tail and laps up the attention, as he's lavished with lots of cuddles.

We introduce ourselves to Antonio, who has been patiently waiting while we all hug Kate, and Vanessa and Leon stroke Henry into the floor.

Antonio was born in Nicaragua. His mother bravely moved her family to San Francisco when they were young, and he has lived there ever since. He never stops smiling and is obviously smitten with my sister. He and Kate are the perfect match. Antonio is well built, with broad shoulders, which Kate just reaches. They are a great contrast, with her blonde hair against his dark skin and his large dark eyes set with a round face and short black curly hair.

Antonio hands Leon a baseball glove and bat, and, because Antonio works for a handbag company, Kate promises Vanessa and me free handbags. We all warm to Antonio straight away; he seems like a genuinely nice guy, and the fact that he can provide handbags on tap is just a bonus!

The traffic heading out of San Francisco is at a standstill. We ring ahead to let Mum and Tom know that we're delayed. They are planning to meet us at Kate's apartment in Vacaville. Kate has to work in the morning and so we plan to switch cars and travel the rest of the journey in Tom's van.

Tom, Shelby, Mum, and Dad live within a few miles of each other, in the foothills of the Sierra Mountains. Cameron Park, where Tom and Shelby live, is about another hour's drive from Vacaville.

Tom and Shelby lived in Sacramento when they first got married. They've made several moves since, each time buying a bigger house and moving further up towards the foothills. They are now about an hour's drive away from Lake Tahoe and are actually hoping to move there once Sam has gone off to college. Like all my brothers, Tom is a carpenter by trade although coupled with his very artistic flair makes bespoke furniture and works as a cabinetmaker. Shelby is a private investigator and although she works out of an office, the nature of the job means that she is always dashing off somewhere, usually to interview someone.

By the time we reach Kate's apartment, it's almost 5.00 p.m., and although we are feeling a bit worse for wear, having been awake for what seems like days, we are beyond excited to see Mum and Tom.

They all flew to England the previous summer for a family wedding, so it's been a whole year since we've seen each other.

Vacaville is scorching hot when we arrive into the parking lot. Kate's apartment is in the second floor of a beautiful, big, Victorian style building, standing on the corner, just outside downtown Vacaville.

We jump out of the car and run over to Mum and Tom.

'Thought it was about time we visited,' I say jokingly to Tom.

'Good to see you, Sis,' he replies, hugging me.

Tom and I have been close since childhood. Growing up, we were like two peas in a pod, and only being thirteen months apart in age and sharing similar facial features, when we were younger were often mistaken for being twins. He is, however, much darker skinned than I am and has very dark hair. I can remember being on holiday once and some Spanish teenagers shouting over at him, mistaking him for one of the local boys. I, too, was mistaken for being a boy several times, I have to say, thanks to my shockingly short haircuts. Perhaps this was the real reason why people often thought we were twins!

Apart from the odd scuffle when we were younger (I was a baton twirling majorette and smacked him clean over the head with my steel baton once during an argument), we were best friends, right through to our teenage years up until the point he met Shelby and left for California. Although 5,000 miles usually sits between us, we have remained close, and he has come to my rescue on more occasions than I can even count.

Nostalgic is a good word to describe Tom, that and a little eccentric, maybe. He is one of the most intelligent people I know and has a lot more common sense than most people I know too. He is also funny and reminds me of Jim Carrey (or maybe Jim Carrey reminds me of Tom), just in the way he seems to make a joke out of everything and has that unique ability to do and say things that makes everyone laugh.

More hugs and we head up to Kate's apartment. She unlocks the door, and the heat comes billowing out.

'Who forgot the aircon?' Tom asks.

Kate's apartment is hotter than an oven. She makes a quick dash to get everyone cold drinks and comes back out on to the balcony area where we all decide it's better we stay.

Feeling a little more refreshed, we load the cases into Tom's van, say our goodbyes to Kate and Antonio, and set off for Cameron Park.

Tom's van is nothing short of awesome: a 1985 Volkswagen Vanagon, which he bought many years before. In fact, I can't remember when he bought it; he's just always seemed to have it. It reminds me of Scooby Doo although the van in that show is blue, Tom's is tan: a tan van.

It has undergone major van surgery in that it's had a Jetta engine conversion, making it more powerful. We are all amazed at his latest modifications, which he's been making over the past few months in preparation for the camping trip. He's taken out the two seated middle bench and replaced it with a rear facing jump seat with custom built cabinetry. He has also replaced all the carpet and seat covers, and it looks just amazing.

I am not sure when Tom's love for Volkswagens began, but he has always liked older or classic cars, and my dad does too so maybe it runs in the family. I remember him having a bright, yellow Morris Minor van, which I think he did a few things to make it roadworthy. I secretly hope this one is roadworthy because we are going to be driving a very long way in it.

We arrive in Cameron Park to our third and final welcome of the day from Dad, Shelby, and Sam. Tom and Shelby have a whole variety of pets that are also there to welcome us; their most recent addition in the form of a rag doll cat called Dave, which is actually called Simon, but Tom likes to refer to it as Dave. Get your head around that.

Tom and Shelby live in a big house, which is set at the foot of a hillside, so it is elevated from the road. It's 2,700 square feet in total with a large entrance room, which Tom has turned into his games room with a pool table. The dining room and kitchen give way to a huge living room, and there are four big bedrooms and three bathrooms. Tom is in the process of landscaping the gardens, but out back, there are some steps that lead up to a fantastic swimming pool, which they had put in shortly after they bought the house. So it's like being at home but on holiday at the same time.

'It's so good to see you all,' Shelby cries, hugging us all together. 'I'm not going to let you leave this time.'

I laugh. 'I wouldn't argue with that.'

Knowing how much I love California, Shelby is very keen for us to move over and likes having us stay with them. She also loves nothing more than being home with her family around her. Sam was a miracle baby, and if she had been given the chance, I think she would have liked to have had a few more children.

She is without question one of the best cooks I know, and we are all looking forward to some of her dinners, Vanessa, especially, who suddenly eats everything going when Shelby is cooking it!

Shelby is ten years elder than Tom and always jokes that she spent so many years being single because she was waiting for Tom to get old enough. She is kind, considerate, empathetic, and shares Tom's dry sense of humour.

We are all so tired that it isn't long before we go to bed. Sam made a banner for each of our rooms, which hangs on the wall opposite my bed. I look over at it as my eyelids start to close, and I drift off to sleep . . . Welcome to California.

Ashtanga Yoga

One of the most exciting things for me about this whole trip to California is that I am going to be practising Ashtanga yoga with a Pattabhi Jois (pronounced patt-ar-bi joyce), authorised Ashtanga yoga teacher. Perhaps it would be helpful if I introduce Ashtanga yoga to you here and explain a little more about what a Pattabhi Jois teacher is, and why I am so excited about it.

To someone who doesn't know much about yoga, the physical practice probably just looks like a sequence of exercises, which in Ashtanga yoga are performed quite quickly and rhythmically. Apart from the fact that it gives you a very lean and toned body, it makes you feel calm and centred and almost like you feel clearer about who you are and what you are doing. Having lived the life I have, that's quite an amazing thing! It's a bit like charging your batteries every morning so you feel fresher inside and out, and it makes your day just flow better and leaves you feeling much happier about yourself and life in general. Interested . . . ?

Ashtanga yoga is an ancient system of yoga which derives from a text known as the Yoga Korunta taught by Vamana Rishi. The legendary Sri Tirumali Krishnamacharya, who was (he died in 1998 when he was 100 years old!) one of the greatest yogis of modern times, was taught this yoga system from his guru, Rama Mohan Brahmachari. (I know these names are a nightmare to read, but I feel compelled to mention the origins of this ancient yoga I am devoted to and practise, and in any case, you'll laugh at yourself, trying to read them!)

Ashtanga vinyasa yoga, as it is often referred to, is a set sequence of postures which are practised and progressed over time. Vinyasa (breath and movement) tristhana, asana (posture), Ujjayi (victorious breath), drishti (gaze or looking place) and bandhas (locks or energy seals) are all fundamental components of the practice. The continuous vinyasa flow of Ashtanga yoga generates heat in the body which cleanses and detoxifies the system, eliminating toxins through sweat, which is generated during the practice.

There are six series in total: primary series, intermediate series, and advanced series A, B, C, and D. Ashtanga yoga is a very dynamic and challenging form of yoga. The first series, which is considered to be the most difficult because it is the one you come to as a beginner, purifies the body, the second purifies the nervous system, and the final and subsequent series purify the mind and transcend gravity and impossibility. It can take years just to master the first, primary series!

Sri K. Pattabhi Jois met Krishnamacharya in 1927, when he was just twelve years old, and studied with him for twenty-five years. Until his death in May 2009, Pattabhi Jois had been teaching the same Ashtanga vinyasa yoga method, uninterrupted for sixty-three years!

To ensure the Ashtanga yoga lineage continued, Pattabhi Jois's students were only ever invited to become authorised or certified teachers. Authorised teachers, having to have completed extensive study at the Ashtanga Yoga Institute in Mysore, India, visit no less than four times and are proficient in the primary series. Certified teachers make more than eight annual trips, with over ten years experience of a daily Ashtanga yoga practice, and are proficient in at least the first three series.

When people refer to Ashtanga Yoga Mysore style, it just means as taught at the Ashtanga Yoga Institute, which Pattabhi Jois directed before his death. His grandson Sharath Rangaswamy, who is the only Ashtanga yoga practitioner in the world, proficient in all six series, is now codirector of the institute.

Mysore style is self-directed study, and within the class, each student will be practising at their own level and pace. The teacher oversees all students, helps, and guides each one into particular postures. When students attend the Ashtanga Yoga Institute in Mysore, India, this is the way in which they are taught; hence the name Mysore style.

In the couple of months leading up to the trip, I've been in touch with an authorised teacher who manages a yoga shala (shala means school) in San Francisco. Melissa seems really nice, and we have emailed back and forth a few times. I was all set to give her a call and attend a Mysore style morning class shortly after arriving.

How wonderful that Kate's new boyfriend (hardly new after a year of dating but new to us) lives in San Francisco! Kate said that I was welcome to stay over at Antonio's place the night before I want to go to the yoga class, and everything has seemed just perfect, like I couldn't have planned for it to work out better.

It has, therefore, been a huge surprise when I called Melissa the day after we arrived to ask about going to the Thursday morning class, to discover that she isn't going to be around for the whole summer. I am already beyond nervous about going to my very first Mysore style Ashtanga yoga class, having taught myself the primary series with the help of the great David Swenson, on his DVD that is.

Melissa has assured me that I am in for a real treat because Michael Harvey, one of the few certified Pattabhi Jois teachers in the world, will be flying in to teach for July and August. She has said that she will let him know I am coming and not to worry.

Kate lives in Vacaville, which is about an hour's drive from Antonio's place in San Francisco. We have agreed Tom will drive me to meet Kate half way to Vacaville, and then Kate and I will drive all the way to San Francisco and stay overnight at Antonio's place. The yoga shala is literally right around the corner, and after practice, I can go back to Antonio's place for a shower and breakfast and enjoy the rest of the day in San Francisco. Mum and Dad are going to pick up Vanessa, Leon, and Sam first thing in the morning and meet us.

Sounds like a military operation, but with three different locations, grandparents, brothers, sisters, and children, all doing different things at different times, planning is a must!

I leave my much-loved sun lounger midafternoon, shower, and start to dry my hair. Why was I born with such unruly curly hair? I have often asked myself this question but never really come up with an answer.

I decide that I'll straighten my hair because I can then tie it up, and it won't be spilling all over the place. Sounds ridiculous all this hair planning, but you need to consider my hair for a minute. It's just past my shoulders, and there is lots of it. My hairdresser said she has never come across anyone with so much hair per hair follicle. I am not sure whether that's something to be proud of, but there it is. It's naturally very curly and kind of just grows out rather than down. Imagine if you will the top of a tree, and you can kind of get the shape of my hair going on in your mind. Surprisingly, it straightens pretty well, considering how unruly it is, but it takes some time and by the end of it, I feel like my head has been part boiled.

'Perfect!' I say to myself, smoothing my hair down one last time while admiring my tan in the mirror before switching off the straighteners.

I say my goodbyes to the kids and give them instructions on behaving saying I'll meet them in San Francisco the following morning. To be honest, I think they are more interested in the royal spoiling they are going to get from Aunt Shelby than missing me for the night.

Shelby then gives me strict instructions on keeping my eyes pealed for potential suitors. She is just as keen as I am for me to live over here and thinks if I happen to meet someone and fall in love, then it would be the perfect way to do it. Now, I know I've not messed about much in the past but, come on, all that in just under six weeks?

Tom arrives home shortly after, and we head out to meet Kate. She arrives a little late.

'How many times have I told you about meeting me late to pick up the kids, Kate?' Tom asks in a stern voice, pretending they are meeting in the parking lot as parents exchanging their child.

We laugh, and feeling excited, I jump into Kate's car, looking forward to the whole experience.

We drive on to San Francisco and get an early night.

I wake up just before 5.30 a.m. and get dressed, deciding shorts are probably going to be my best option. I look in the mirror and feel thankful that my hair is still straight and then tie it back in a ponytail.

Kate emerges from the bedroom and says she is going to take Henry out before we leave.

She returns shortly afterwards to find me pacing the living room. I am feeling quite nervous at the thought of my first ever Mysore style Ashtanga class. Kate reads my mind.

'You'll be fine, Grace. Stop worrying, you'll love it,' she says reassuringly.

'I know I will, I just feel nervous about going to my first ever class and meeting this world-renowned teacher.'

Kate smiles and gives me a hug.

She has always been a protective sister being five years elder, but as we have grown up, the age gap has closed, and we have become more like best friends. I still look up to her, and she inspires me enormously. She is so positive and always has so much energy, drive, and enthusiasm.

'I have something for you,' Kate says. 'A kind of welcome to California yoga type gift.' She smiles, gets up, and goes into the bedroom.

Not surprisingly Kate owns more handbags than probably anyone you have ever known. My mum, Shelby, and I have joked with her about how awesome it is that she has landed herself a boyfriend who works for a handbag company. She now has an entire wardrobe of handbags in her guest room. Literally, a whole closet full, each one hanging perfectly on the many wooden rails or sitting on shelves. She chooses a new bag every day to match her outfit.

Kate emerges with a gorgeous brightly decorated canvas bag with the words peace and nature written all over it: just perfect for yoga.

I squeal with excitement 'Thank you! I love it!' I say quickly, taking the things out of my own bag and putting them into the new one. 'I've been here a couple of days and already I have two new bags.'

'Get used to it,' Kate says. 'You'll never have to buy another bag again.'

'Fantastic, can you get him to branch out into shoes?'

We both laugh, pack the remainder of our bags, check we have everything we need, and head out.

Kate has this great satnav called Emily (don't ask me why because I have no idea, but everyone seems to name their satnav. Tom and Shelby's is called 'crack lady' because she sends them all over the place and so they say she is on crack), who directs us straight to our destination (obviously not on crack then).

The yoga place is located behind a yellow door on a sloping street. I say sloping because in San Francisco, there's sloping and there's just plain steep to the point where you could easily walk up the street on all fours. We park right outside, and I sit staring at the door, wondering what the hell I am going to find behind it. I have no idea what to expect and feel so nervous that I think the butterflies might just pop right out of my mouth and flutter away.

'Should I go ring the bell?' I ask Kate nervously.

'Well, my car clock is always four minutes fast, so wait another few minutes and then go,' Kate suggests. 'Ooh, I wonder what he's like,' she says excitedly.

'Oh, Kate, stop! I am nervous enough as it is.'

Just then, a man emerges from the neighbouring door, punches a code in the keypad by the door, and goes in.

'That must be him!' I exclaim, grabbing my bag and yoga mat ready to go.

'Text me when you're done, and I'll come pick you up,' Kate says. 'And stop worrying. You'll love it!' She smiles.

Easy for her to say, she isn't the one about to go through the yellow door!

It's almost 6.30 a.m. and freezing. I get out of the car, and I feel my legs shaking. I wonder whether that's from the cold or whether they are going to buckle under the pressure. I knock nervously on the door and then quickly turn back around to pull a face at Kate, who is still waiting in the car.

Michael Harvey opens the door, and I wave to Kate as I go in.

I can't help the smile that suddenly appears on my face. I didn't realise yoga teachers were so handsome. I think I have handsome on the brain!

'Hi, you must be Michael, I'm Grace, from England,' I say, extending my hand. 'I think Melissa was going to talk to you about me.' I am so nervous it feels as though my words are falling over themselves.

Michael Harvey is dreamy: tall, with an athletic build, dark brown hair, which is cropped short, and piercing blue eyes, which twinkle and make it appear as though he is smiling even when he isn't. His nose is perfectly straight, not too big and not too small, and he has full lips, which turn up at the sides, again making it appear as though he is smiling. He's wearing dark blue baggy sweats with a white T-shirt that has an *om* symbol on the front. He doesn't really look like a yoga teacher, but then again, my only experience of male yoga teachers to this point has been sagely looking Indian teachers, and he is far from sagely looking!

'Yes, she did, hi,' he says, warmly shaking my hand and then asks about my practice.

I explain that I have been practising Hatha yoga since 2007, then began practising Ashtanga yoga in August 2008, and have pretty much taught myself the primary series, and so I'm very keen to practice Mysore style.

'I am just here for six weeks, visiting my family and staying a few hours drive away, so I'm hoping to come and practise a few more times while I am here,' I say, feeling in total awe of the fact that I am going to practise under the guidance of a certified Ashtanga yoga teacher.

I've spent the past year, hoping that one day I would find a teacher and although it is only going to be for a few practices, unless I go to the Ashtanga Yoga Institute in India (which at this point in my life I am not able to do), it can't get much better than this!

The shala has a distinct eastern feel to it, with a picture of a Hindu God next to a couple of framed photographs of Pattabhi Jois and Tirumali Krishnamacharya (however you pronounce them is just fine!) adorning the walls, and the wonderful musty smell of incense fills the air. Although it's chilly outside and the floor is tiled, the entrance room feels warm. I sit down on the cushioned window seats to the right of the room and take off my trainers and jacket. The room is basic and earthy but feels homely and inviting. Opposite me and to the left of the room is a wooden unit constructed for students' shoes and bags and a whole shelf of Mysore style cotton rugs. To the front of the room is a low wooden cupboard, which has more units for shoes, bags, and mats. On top, a framed photograph of Sharath and his daughter sits proudly next to a few yoga magazines and the register with a glass pot for drop-in fees. I stand up and put my things in one of the empty wooden units.

Michael says I can go through and either make a start or wait for him to come into the room. I decide to go through and set up my mat and wait for him. I wonder if I will manage to practise because my knees feel so weak from feeling nervous. Now am I nervous about the practice or about him? I wonder. Focus! I tell myself sternly.

I walk through the doorway to the left of the entrance room. To my right is a small bathroom and to the left another doorway covered by a dark red velvet curtain, which I move to the side and walk through. The smell of incense is inviting, and it feels even warmer as I walk through the corridor, which then becomes another small open room to my right. Steps to my left lead down to a small narrow room where a few people have already set up and are busy practising. I make my way down the five steps. The floor is black and seems soft and springy under my feet, and I guess it is some kind of flooring designed especially for yoga practice, either that or just soft flooring! At the end of the room is a tall frosted window the width of the room, and the walls around me are whitewashed, featuring more black and white photographs of Krishnamacharya, Pattabhi Jois, and his grandson, Sharath Rangaswamy in various yoga poses hung as though they are there to watch over and encourage your practice themselves.

Nervously I fumble about with my mat, trying to get it straight, wondering why it is such a huge issue, and then wait for Michael to arrive.

A few minutes later, I find myself standing with my hands in prayer position chanting *om*, desperately trying to remember the opening Sanskrit prayer (Sanskrit is thought to be the oldest language in the world and the language of yoga). I am suddenly propelled back to primary school when we would say the Lord's Prayer before assembly began and which for some time I could never remember.

As Michael chants each verse, I mumble the Sanskrit words and just hope that in between my muffled mumbles, it sounds somewhat like Sanskrit, either that or he just thinks I am a mad mumbling English woman, but then again he probably thinks that anyway.

I look around. The other students seem to know their Sanskrit prayer by heart, and I decide that I am going to learn the opening and closing prayers by heart.

I begin my practice and soon forget about being nervous, that is until Michael comes over to adjust my posture or suggest something. He has the most sparkly blue eyes I have ever seen, and his voice is very rhythmic and gentle. I am mesmerised, but it totally throws me off when he speaks to me, and I just find myself smiling and giggling like a school girl. At several points, I actually also forget where I am in the primary series and practise a couple of postures out of sequence. This causes him to correct me that only then leads to another bumbling error because of giggling or being mesmerised by his sparkly eyes.

Despite this, for the most part, I am totally focused in my practice and realise for the first time that the absolute key to Ashtanga yoga is vinyasa: creating heat in the body and sweating, which makes getting into the postures easier! I have never sweat like this in my entire life, and I think how absolutely ridiculous it was to have straightened my hair yesterday. It is now as wet from sweat as it would be had I just got out of the shower, and my entire body is dripping in sweat. Sounds gross I know, but it's just amazing. I'm achieving the postures so much easier than I have ever done before, and as Michael makes adjustments and pushes me further into postures, I realise that I am going to learn more in these few practice sessions than I have learnt in months of my own practice.

I'm attempting the womb embryo posture. This posture in its full expression has eluded me to this point. It involves getting into full lotus position (which is the classic yogi posture with legs crossed and each foot placed on the opposite thigh) and then putting your arms through your legs up to the elbows before resting your hands on your chin. You then hold this position for five breaths and roll back and up again, rotating each time so that you turn full circle. I can manage the full lotus position but there is no way my arms will go through my legs, let alone up to the elbows! Michael comes by and hands me a spray bottle.

'Wet your legs,' he says, rather matter of factly.

I can feel the blood rush to my cheeks as I begin to blush. Wet my legs! What on God's earth is he talking about and isn't it all rather a bit inappropriate, wetting my legs honestly! You can tell I'm English, can't you?

He must have seen the look on my face.

'If you wet your legs, then you can just slip your arms right through,' he says smiling down at me before walking off.

'Right you are then,' I say out loud, spraying down my legs.

With my legs now dripping wet, my arms do indeed push right on through, up to the elbows! If my hands were free, I might do a bit of an 'oh yay' dance with my arms waving around in the air, but I can't because they are slipped tightly through my legs. Although they have gone through very easily, I am now wondering how the hell they are going to come out.

I struggle to roll back and forth, and as I roll back, I stay in that position. Now I know what one of those ladybird bugs feels like when it falls helplessly on its back, rolling around on its shell. I am a sodding living ladybird!

Michael comes back over and physically rolls me back and forth until I come round in complete circle. Somehow (I have no idea how) I manage to take the whole weight of my body onto my hands and move into the cock posture. Seriously, that's what it's called, and I thought the same thing when I first heard it, so no further comment required.

I move through my practice with renewed confidence at having just managed to get my arms up to their elbows through my legs.

When I finish, I go through to the upper room to rest. I feel as if I am floating on a cloud, and in between feeling elated about my yoga practice, I can't stop the teenage girl with a crush-like thoughts swimming around in my head. I brush the thoughts aside once more and resume focusing on my breath as I try to relax, my heart racing in my chest. This is one of the most amazing experiences of my life, and I can't stop smiling.

I quickly ring Kate and whisper that I am done, before rolling up my mat and catching Michael's attention before I leave.

He walks up the steps to greet me. 'You did a great job today, Grace, and I was surprised at how far you have got with your practice, teaching yourself,' he says.

I feel myself blush as my heart seems to pump faster at the mere sound of his voice. Yes, definite teenage girl crush.

'Thanks, I really love yoga,' I say, hoping that perhaps he thinks my cheeks are burning so brightly because I am hot from practising.

'Well, I should get back to class. I'll see you when you come next time.'

My heart feels like it will burst. I thank him again and hold my hands in prayer and bow my head. He returns the gesture and smiles.

I think I might actually faint at this point but manage to steady myself against the wall as I watch him return to the class.

I feel truly blessed to have met him and not for the reason you are now thinking either! Yes, he is devastatingly good looking, with eyes that are like diamonds dancing on the ocean, but those eyes also offer a glimpse of a warm-hearted, strong, soul filled with love, light, and goodness. Okay, total rubbish; I fancy the yoga pants off him, but I do feel connected to him through yoga with a huge sense of respect and awe for his position as my teacher for the next few weeks. Question is whether I can keep the enormous crush I have on him intact enough to actually focus on practising!

I buy myself a Mysore cotton rug and race outside to meet Kate.

'Well?' she asks impatiently. 'Was it good?'

'Oh, Kate!' I gush. 'It was just amazing. Look at my hair!' I say as I wipe my hand across my soaking wet hair. 'I have never sweated so much in my life. It was the best experience ever.'

I relay the whole experience back to her, filling her in on all the new things I learnt in just one practice.

'Oh, and he has the most sparkly eyes you have ever seen!' I finish up by saying.

Kate chuckles. 'Is he single then?' she enquires curiously.

'I don't know,' I reply. 'I think he's gay.'

'Why do you think that?'

'Not a clue, just do.'

We both fall about laughing.

Good News and Bad News

The whole day following the Ashtanga yoga practice is spent floating on a yoga cloud. I am overwhelmed with such a sense of calm and peacefulness that I have never felt before. My body feels amazing; stretched, energised, toned . . . and tanned!

After arriving back at Antonio's apartment, we head down to La Boulange, a great restaurant on the same street for breakfast. We sit outside and enjoy the most delicious yoghurt, fruit, and granola breakfast bowl I have ever eaten.

'I think I would benefit from yoga,' Antonio announces.

'Everyone would benefit from yoga,' I reply enthusiastically. Being the yoga ambassador I am, I never tire of talking about it.

'I think it would help my breathing a bit because my nose is always blocked,' Antonio says taking a deep breath and making a funny nasal sound. 'See, I sound like a horse.'

Kate laughs. 'No, you don't, honey,' she says, cuddling up to him.

'You could try some breathing techniques that help to cleanse your nadis,' I suggest.

'I didn't know I had any nadis but will take your word for it,' Antonio says, looking puzzled.

'Nadis are the energy channels in your body. You can't see them, but they are very much a part of your body, as, say, are your arms and legs,' I say, continuing. 'Prana, which means life force, pervades all living things in the universe and enters the body through the avenue of the breath and circulates throughout the nadis within the body. Basically, the more the free flowing the prana is within the body, the healthier a person you'll be,' I explain.

'Wow!' exclaims Antonio. 'You learn something new everyday. Did you know you had nadis?' he says, turning to Kate.

'Not a clue, nada,' Kate says, making Antonio laugh.

'See, you are learning some Spanish,' he says. Antonio who can speak fluent Spanish has been trying to teach Kate for some time, but she says she sounds like a demented robot and so won't continue even attempting to learn.

'Hardly,' she says, laughing.

'Nadi shodhana is a breathing technique. Nadi, as I said, means energy channel, and shodhana means cleansing. In English, you would call it alternate nostril breathing. Basically it balances the energy on the left and right sides of your body. You may notice sometimes during the day that your nose feels blocked on the right side and then later in the day you might notice it switches to the left side.'

Antonio and Kate listen intently as I explain how nadi shodhana works.

'There are three main energy channels in the body. Sushumna is the main nadi running up the centre of the body.' I indicate with my finger, running up the centre of my body. 'Ida nadi runs the left side and is related to cool moon energy and pingala runs the right side and is related to warm sun energy. Nadi shodhana balances and cleanses the energy flow between both the right and left nadis.'

'This is fascinating,' Kate says. 'A whole new world of information and things that we never even knew existed!' she says, amazed. 'So how do we do it?' she asks excitedly, bringing her chair closer.

I give them a quick instruction of the nadi shodhana technique, which simply regulates the breath through one nostril at a time.

They both sit with their eyes closed, breathing in through one nostril, holding the breath in, and breathing out through the other nostril.

A few people stroll by and smile, giving Kate and Antonio a second glance as they walk by.

'That's amazing,' Antonio says, opening his eyes.

He takes a full deep breath in. 'I am going to keep trying that. It really works!'

'Of course, it works!' I exclaim. 'Yoga doesn't come from the oldest wisdom in the world for nothing, you know,' I say, feeling pleased that it's helped Antonio.

'I feel really calm now,' Kate says. 'I might start doing that when I get stressed at work.'

'You should. It's a great stress buster.'

Just then we hear Dad's whistle. Ever since we were little, he has always done this very distinct 'wolf whistle'. Whenever any of us have been separated in shops or are meeting up, he'll whistle. Over the years, we've all adopted the whistle for finding each other while we're out.

Dad's the pack leader (or the max jaffa as he used to tell us when we were younger) and so naturally has the loudest whistle!

Vanessa and Leon come running over and both give me a hug.

'How was yoga, Mum?' Vanessa says.

'Fab! Really amazing! I loved it,' I reply, my thoughts once again returning to Michael Harvey.

'Sounds lovely, Mum, I bet you want to go again,'

'Yes, I do. I hope I can go a few more times while we are here. I have to make the most of it.'

'Anyway, enough about me. How are you both, what have you been up to?'

Leon smiles. 'Lots, Mum. We had a great time,' he says.

'Don't tell Mum about the Oreos,' Vanessa whispers to Leon.

'We had a whole box of Oreos, in bed!' Leon pipes up.

Vanessa playfully wraps her arms around his shoulders and holds her hand over his mouth.

'Ssssh, silly, or she won't go again,' she says, giggling.

I laugh. Although I don't mind them having treats, I can be a little strict with healthy eating.

'Aunt Shelby says we are on vacation and so we are allowed,' Leon says, looking delighted at the prospect of lots more goodies coming his way.

'Well, just as long as you enjoyed them,' I say, giving Leon another hug.

We spend the day in San Francisco, walk the length of Pier 39, do some shopping, and generally enjoy being tourists.

We visit Chrissy Fields and the Golden Gate Bridge. We walk up to the museum which sits underneath the bridge, and it's absolutely freezing. Despite it being in the nineties and hundreds in Vacaville and Cameron Park, San Francisco can get pretty chilly during the summer. Mark Twain summed it up nicely when he said 'the coldest winter I ever spent was a summer in San Francisco'. Kate and Antonio inform me that the official

San Francisco summer is actually more in September and October and even gets warmer in the spring than it does during the usual summer months.

Dad does the usual and disappears. It happens wherever we go, one minute he's there and the next he has gone, wandering. I dread to think what's going to happen when he gets a little older and senility sets in (it's an inevitability for him I'm afraid) and really begins to wander off, he'll end up in another state or something!

Welcoming the warmth of our cars, we decide to drive out to Golden Gate Park. I've seen models in yoga magazines having their photographs taken in Golden Gate Park, and I'm thrilled at the prospect of being able to do the same. Hardly a model but it seems quite cool all the same.

'Let's do some yoga,' I say as we head into the park.

We stop by some enormous trees and make our way across the grass. Kate and I do the warrior II posture, downward and upward dog postures, and then I get her to take some photographs of me in the dancer posture, which is my favourite yoga pose. I think of how great they'll look in front of a huge Cypress tree.

On the way back to the car, Mum does some funny-looking poses, which are a hilarious take on what we have been doing. It's so funny that we all laugh hysterically as we get back into the cars.

What a perfect end to a perfect day!

We make the two-hour drive back and find Shelby cooking dinner as we come through the door. I give her a hug.

'So?' she says, looking up from chopping potatoes, 'How was it? I got your text about the gorgeous Mr Michael Harvey. Tell me more,' she says excitedly.

As Shelby is very encouraging of me to meet 'Mr Right' this summer, any mention of liking someone kicks her private eye skills into overdrive.

'Well, I think he is gay actually,' I say rather nonchalantly.

'Gay? What makes you think that?' she says, looking puzzled. 'Did you ask him, did he tell you?'

'Well, no, he didn't, but I think he is.'

'You mean you have no idea, and you have just jumped to some conclusion to make him unavailable to you,' she says. 'Grace, you have to put yourself out there, make him know you are available, and then he'll pick up on the vibe and won't be able to help himself. You are a great catch!'

The following morning after my dawn Ashtanga practice, I find Shelby dismantling the coffee machine.

'It's gone funny again. The light came on part way through, giving me a latte and now it's stopped. I think it needs cleaning,' she says, craning her neck so she can peer into the machine.

Tom and Shelby have a very state-of-the-art coffee machine. You just have to fill the water jug, switch it on, and insert your packet choice. Shelby has every single style of coffee going from French Vanilla to Espresso and you can choose from Latte to Skinny Cap. She even has green tea and hot chocolate. It's like having a permanent Starbucks in your kitchen. It does, however, need some maintaining, usually just a clean through so it's working as good as new again.

The machine whirrs into life again as Shelby inserts a new latte parcel.

'Want one?' she says, turning to me.

'No need to ask. Of course, I do,' I say, laughing. I can't get enough of the stuff. My two cups a morning is steadily increasing to three and four.

'Better make it a Skinny Cap though, otherwise I'll be mooing by Friday.'

Shelby chuckles.

'Forget about coffee. I have some good news and some bad news.'

'Come on then,' I say, intrigued. 'Don't keep me in suspense.'

'Well, the good news is Michael isn't gay, but the bad news is he's married.'

I'm not sure which news I like best.

'How on earth do you know that?' I say, bewildered.

'It's my job to investigate. I couldn't help myself. I just wanted to know if there's a chance for you with him. Now there isn't, you can move on,' she says.

I laugh. 'I can't believe you. I tell you I like someone, and then as if by some fairy godmother magic, I wake up in the morning and you have researched him!'

'Well, hardly illegal. It's public knowledge. I just did some Internet research, but the point is, at least you know and won't get hung up on him and keep wondering whether he is an option for you.'

She has a point.

'True,' I say. 'I completely respect the fact that he is married and will leave well enough alone. Probably a good thing anyway, considering he is my teacher while I am here,' I say, convincing myself further.

I think about Michael for a second . . . those eyes.

'It's the sparkly eyes, isn't it?' Shelby says, as if reading my mind.

I smile.

'See, there you go again, with your Shelby PI intuition.'

We laugh and sit down to drink our morning coffee.

Cool

Tom works a four-day week, and so with the following day being Friday, his day off, we decide that rather than hang out by the pool, we'll go for a hike. If we leave early enough, we can be back before the midday sun starts to kick in and we blister in the heat.

'Do we have to go?' Sam asks as Tom packs up a cooler bag.

'Yes, Sam, we do,' Tom says. 'You'll enjoy it, and Grace, Vanessa, and Leon are only here for a while, so it's good we take them out and show them around a bit.'

Sam protests. 'But it's so hot, and I really hate hiking.'

Sam is somewhat of a gifted child and excels at pretty much everything. He's always coming up with ideas for wacky inventions, and I have no doubt he will grow into one of those people who invent something that takes the world by storm and become so wealthy from that one thing that they can then pretty much do whatever they please for the rest of their lives. That'll be Sam.

He is, however, very much an indoor rather than outdoor kind of boy. He isn't overly keen on outdoor activities, and his pet hates are walking and cycling.

I think after a near miss on his bike once he is convinced it's now possessed, although I think the fact that one of his favourite novels, Stephen King's *Christine*, probably has something to do with that notion.

Tom, on the other hand, is very much an outdoor kind of person and loves nothing more than being out in the middle of nowhere, climbing, hiking, running, or generally being active. As he usually has Fridays off, he'll often drag Sam outdoors, encouraging him (against his will) to be more active.

Shelby is working and has left early. We aim to be out of the house and on our way by 8.00 a.m.

Vanessa and Leon are busy tying their trainer laces together and trying to have a three-legged race down the hallway with Dave skipping at their heels, trying to eat the trailing laces.

Inevitably, they end up rolling over and falling into a heap in the dining room, with poor Dave underneath.

'Five minutes!' Tom shouts.

Sam groans. 'But, Dad!' he protests, making one last attempt to talk Tom out of bringing him along.

'It'll only be for a couple of hours. Now come on,' Tom says, grabbing the cooler bag and making his way towards the door.

We manage to untie Vanessa and Leon's laces and are all buckled up in the van by eight five.

'Not bad at all,' says Tom, turning on his iPod.

Culture Club's 'Sweet Toxic Love' blasts through the speakers.

Tom has an eclectic taste in music, and we are all busy compiling playlists, which we've added to every time we hear another song we like.

Tom has his work cut out for him in the last few weeks of our trip, making all these playlists up for us to transfer on to our iPods.

'So where are we heading then?' I ask as we hit countryside.

'Auburn SRA,' Tom replies. 'That's State Recreational Area. It's a good place to hike and remember that film, *Triple X*, where Vin Diesel jumps off the bridge, well, a stuntman who looks like Vin Diesel?' he says, turning to look at me.

'Yes! I watched that film. He steals the red Corvette and then drives it off a bridge, jumping out with a parachute on.'

'Well, that bridge is in the park,' Tom says.

'How cool!' I say excitedly.

After a forty-minute drive, we round a corner and the bridge comes into view.

'Wouldn't fancy jumping off that myself,' I say, thinking how much higher it looks now we are seeing the real thing.

'I would,' Tom says.

Sam rolls his eyes.

'Yes and no doubt coercing me into it,' he says.

'What does coercing mean?' Vanessa says.

'It means,' Sam says, 'that because he is my dad, he says I have to do something, even if I don't want to do it.'

'Well, that's not very nice, Uncle Tom, making Sam jump off that bridge,' Vanessa says, taking it all very literally.

Tom smiles. 'I wouldn't make you jump off the bridge, Sam, but think a bungee jump off there would be kind of cool.'

'Well, you're on your own there,' I say, looking up again at the bridge.

We park up by the river and walk down the rocky slope towards the water. The bridge looms to the right of us.

'We'll head up river,' Tom says, 'and then go up a little higher and catch a trail,' he says, looking up to where a trail moves higher and away from the river.

Tom has a camel pack.

'Anyone like water before we head off?'

'Yes!' Sam cries. 'I'd rather sit here with it though and wait for you to come back,' he says.

'No chance, come on,' Tom coaxes.

We clamber over the rocks along the shallower part of the river as we head up stream.

Tom climbs up and over several rocks until he ends up towards the middle of the river.

I get the camera out and take some photos of us all by the water.

I hear the splash first and quickly turn around to see Tom's head pop up out of the water.

'*Freezing!*' he yells.

Considering it's getting into the eighties already, it's hard to imagine that the water can be cold, but the American River is hardly Caribbean waters. The forks of the river that run through the park are shallow in places with sharp jagged rocks but where Tom has fallen in, fortunately it's deeper.

Sam laughs the hardest, seeing that somehow karma has repaid him for being dragged out hiking in the heat.

Tom takes it all in his stride.

'Well, at least I'll stay cool in the heat and am sure after half an hour of hiking, I'll be as dry as a bone,' he says positively.

Fortunately, Sam still has the backpack and so Shelby's prized camera is safe.

'So glad I didn't have that backpack on,' Tom says, echoing my thoughts.

We follow a dripping wet Tom up the trail where I am sure it feels hotter because it's higher.

We've been hiking along the trail now for about thirty minutes.

Leon screams, 'Snake!'

We're all walking in a line with Leon in the middle. Somehow he manages to lag behind and is now staring at a rattlesnake, which is a few feet to the side of him, obviously trying to find shade.

'Don't move,' Tom says, lowering his voice and stepping quietly towards Leon, who is now stuck fast to the spot clearly in shock. His arms are rigid by his sides and his fingers splayed out as if playing musical statues.

I feel sick.

'Don't scream or make a sound,' Tom whispers to Leon. 'You're much bigger than the snake, and it is going to want to get away from you as much as you want to get away from it.'

'If we give him some space, he won't bother you. Now, carefully and as calmly as you can, walk over towards me,' Tom says, reaching out his hand towards Leon.

Leon does exactly as Tom instructs and grabs his hand.

'Just keep walking,' Tom says.

We walk further up the trail and stop.

I let out the breath I feel I have been holding in since I first saw the snake and grab Leon.

'Are you okay?' I say, hugging him tightly.

He shrugs his shoulders and his lower lip wobbles.

'I think so,' he says, hugging me back.

'I knew this was a bad idea,' Sam says. 'Hiking and cycling can only lead to some disaster.'

'No, it won't,' Tom says. 'Just one of those things, and we'll probably never encounter another rattlesnake again ever.'

'Well, I hope not,' Vanessa says, stepping closer to Tom.

'Me neither,' Leon says.

'Well, I'd rather come face to face with a rattlesnake than a black bear or a mountain lion,' Tom says.

'That's helpful, Tom,' I say sarcastically. 'Do you think we could leave now?'

'That's the best thing anyone has said all morning,' Sam says.

'You mean there are bears and lions here too?' Vanessa cries.

'They do live in the park, but no one ever encounters them on the trails,' Tom says.

'Well, let's not be the first,' I say.

'Hang on before you go racing back down the trail,' Tom says. 'Let's just find somewhere to sit for five or ten minutes and give that snake a chance to find some shade before we head back down.'

'Yes, Mummy, let's wait,' Leon says, sounding relieved that he doesn't have to go back straight the way to the spot where he had seen the snake.

We walk further up the trail and find a small clearing that looks out across the valley and the river below. We are at least a 100 feet up from the river and towards the edge the path just falls away to a steep slope and trees below, running down to the river.

'Be careful,' I instruct Vanessa and Leon.

We sit and drink some more water before deciding that the snake will have now probably found some shade to crawl beneath. Tom informs us that rattlesnakes sometimes sun themselves in the middle of a trail but generally are looking for somewhere to hide.

'Leon, you hold my hand and walk up front with me,' Tom says. 'Vanessa, you walk behind us, then you, Sam and Grace, you take the rear.'

'Great, so I get bitten on the bum,' I say, only half joking.

'Rather you than me,' Sam says.

'We'll be fine,' Tom says, 'now let's go.'

We walk back down the trail, quickening our pace as we pass the spot where Leon saw the snake. Just as Tom said, there is no sign of him, obviously having crawled underneath one of the big boulders at the side of the trail.

We make it back to the van, and I feel relieved that we are soon to be safely on our way back to Cameron Park.

'We can come back again next Friday if you like,' Tom suggests.

'You're on your own there, Tom,' I say. 'Thanks though, for knowing what to do and getting Leon out of there.'

'Rattlesnakes usually get out of the way of humans if they can and only bite if they are really startled or provoked,' Tom explains.

'Well, I'm surprised Leon's high-pitched scream wasn't enough to provoke it.'

'For whatever reason it didn't, thank God, and because he was quite a few feet away, I guess the snake didn't feel threatened,' Tom says.

As we drive away from Auburn SRA, Sam hooks up the PlayStation® for Leon, and he soon forgets all about his snake encounter, immersed instead in Lego® Star Wars.

We pull up at a stop sign.

'Look, a proper Coca-Cola® truck, just like the one on the advert,' Vanessa says, pointing at the truck that had pulled up in the gas station at the side of the road.

I take a photo. There's a green sign just to the right of us. It reads:

Cool

POP 2,250 ELEV 1,518

'That's never the name of this place,' I say to Tom.

'Yes, it is, cool huh?' Tom says.

I laugh.

'Yes, that's totally cool, a place called Cool.'

Garage Yoga

Traditionally, yoga is practised before dawn, around 4.30 a.m. I've always been an early riser, but usually early has meant around 6.00 a.m. Last year I read a great book called *The Monk Who Sold His Ferrari* by Robin Sharma. Fantastic book, great story, but back to my early mornings, in this book, he suggests that 5.00 a.m. is holy hour and that this time of day is like no other. I tried it and have been hooked to getting up at 5.00 a.m. ever since. It's unbelievably quiet at 5.00 a.m. (obviously, if you live in a big city, it might not be, but where I live, everyone else is sleeping), and in terms of yoga and certainly according to the great Pattabhi Jois, early morning is the correct time to practise.

Your body is refreshed and your mind, still and quiet from sleeping. Although in the afternoon you feel more flexible and energetic, you are also full of the day's activities and have eaten. It's the dawn of a new day and nothing sets you up for that better than yoga.

I started practising yoga at 5.00 a.m. about a month before coming to California. Before then, my practice was always during the day, scheduled around work and the kids. Being drawn to the traditional teachings of yoga and particularly those of Pattabhi Jois' system of Ashtanga Yoga, I am keen to establish this early morning practice.

It was hard at first and felt as though my joints needed oiling. I have felt dizzy, almost passed out several times during the first few weeks, and on at least two occasions, have fallen over. Once, I actually crashed into the book shelf, not at all pleasant for me or the book shelf! There were also days when I almost had to force myself to the mat (not the ideal yoga scenario I have to say) but I have persisted and trust that it will get easier. 'Practise and all is coming,' Pattabhi Jois often said.

When I emailed Melissa about the possibility of practising at her shala, I mentioned that I was finding the 5.00 a.m. practice hard. She assured me that it would get easier, and as my practice progresses, it will become as natural as getting up and brushing my teeth.

Although it isn't quite the same as brushing my teeth, by the end of the first month, it did feel easier. I haven't fallen over for a whole week, have actually been getting up with a spring in my step and looking forward to getting on the mat.

An early morning practice tones your body like no other. Like I said, your body is rested, and you haven't eaten anything. Yoga is typically practised on an empty stomach, and it's always best to wait at least ninety minutes after eating before practising. Early morning, therefore, is optimum. Yoga has a beneficial effect on all systems of the body and improves the functioning of these systems, which in just a short space of time becomes noticeable. Since practising at 5.00 a.m., I have felt more energised than ever before and my days flow better as the weeks have passed.

Over time, however, the practice isn't really so much about the physical, more the spiritual and 5.00 a.m. is definitely conducive to that.

Since arriving in California, I have been getting up at my usual 5.00 a.m. and practising yoga on the patio by the pool. It has been difficult to practise in the house because Tom and Shelby's carpet is about two inches deep and so even with the mat, it's like practising yoga on jelly.

The other obstacle is Dave. Remember I mentioned him, the ragdoll cat? I have never in my life met a cat like him. So, as well as calling him Dave instead of Simon, Tom nicknamed him 'Dave the Rave' and 'Party Boy Dave' because, well, he just goes on one and when he does, gets into everything. He is always climbing into something, rolling himself up in something, or generally up to no good.

The other morning, I moved the mat to the tiled kitchen floor but he insisted on trying to ravel himself up in the end of the mat. Then when jumping my feet to my hands in 'downward dog', I sent him reeling across the floor. Fortunately, the water bowl broke his flight but unfortunately it didn't deter him from returning to the mat. Practising yoga with a huge hairy cat is no fun and so I then moved my practice up by the pool. It's warm, even at 5.00 a.m., and still quiet and dark but not too dark that I can't see.

After my first real Mysore-style practice, however, you'll remember I said that I've discovered one of the secrets to Ashtanga yoga is in generating heat in the body, resulting in sweat. When I have practised at home, the room has been warm, but I haven't generated anywhere near as much sweat as I did when I practised at the yoga shala. It's made such a massive difference to my practice, both in terms of how I have felt during and after, and how my body has responded to getting into the postures.

Traditional yoga teachings recommend against practising yoga outside and so continuing my intention to progress my yoga practice, I decide I need to find a new venue, preferably without Dave as my sidekick (no pun intended there either).

Tom suggested the garage. Last night he shifted things about a bit and has given me almost one side to practise in. I am a little concerned about the possibility of coming face to face with a spider, or, worst still, a black widow spider, but Tom has assured me that if there are any in there, they are well hidden in the darkest of corners and won't bother me. He also hooked an air nozzle up to the compressor and cleared the whole area of dust and cobwebs from corners.

Dave is waiting at the door leading from the kitchen to the garage.

'Sorry, Dave, but no yoga for you today,' I say as I lean down to stroke his head. He darts off in the other direction before I get a chance to touch him. He always wants to be in on what's going on, but the minute anyone tries to give him any fuss, let alone pick him up, he makes a run for it.

With the exception of the possibility of there being spiders hidden away, the garage is perfect for yoga. The floor is solid; it's spacious and because there's no air conditioning, it's hot.

I start my practice and after only a few minutes, start to sweat. I can't believe that for almost a year I have been practising Ashtanga yoga without breaking into much of a sweat: such a key part of a successful practice. Still, I know now and after just one practice at the yoga place in San Francisco, I've already learnt so many new things and am eager to learn more.

The thought of practising there returns more thoughts of Michael Harvey swimming around my head. Why is he married? Why is he my teacher for the next few weeks and why now? There always has to be a reason for everything. Why me? The thoughts continue as I try to focus on yoga.

Beginning the seated postures, I fold forward and rest my head on my knees, lifting up to gaze at my toes. I see something move to my left. Oh no! Please don't let that be spider. I turn my head and sure enough scurrying from underneath the tool cabinet is a small black spider. Granted it's small but still a spider, and I can't very well keep practising with a spider running around me. I lean over to get a closer look and to check that it doesn't have the infamous black spot on its back. No, just a harmless (or that's what I need to keep telling myself) black spider.

I'm not petrified of spiders, not in the way some people are, but I don't want to become best friends with them either. I don't feel comfortable with them, and I certainly won't entertain picking one up. Being a true yogi, however, I will never kill one either. What to do?

There's an empty plastic water bottle on top of the cabinet. I stand up, pick it up, and bend down, trying to sweep the spider to the other side of the garage. The sweeping isn't working and unfortunately I squash half its body. Some of its legs are still moving; I have actually paralysed the spider. Why didn't I just let him run along on his merry way instead of bothering him and then squashing him to death, well half to death because half of him seems to still be alive!

Now what to do seems so much more of a pressing dilemma. There's a box of rags on the end of the cabinet, and trying not to look, I pick the spider up in the rag and toss it to the other side of the garage. Out of sight, out of mind, or at least, that's the theory. I feel terrible. I really don't want to squash it again but perhaps I should put it out of its misery.

I take a deep breath. There is nothing more I can do now; it's done.

'Moving on,' I say out loud, returning to the mat.

I resume my practice. I roll into the fish posture, which requires you to lie on your back with your feet in lotus, then arch your back, lift your chest, and drop your head back so that the crown of your head touches the floor. Basically, I am now looking at the garage door, but from an upside down view. Tom has attached a huge Union Jack to the inside of the garage door and dangling from the centre of it, I can see a brown spider. It isn't particularly big or even hairy, but there's something about it which makes me feel uneasy. The thought of having killed one of its far distant cousins springs to mind and perhaps it's coming to seek revenge on behalf of the garage spider population!

I move my gaze above it and try to focus on my breathing. Perhaps the spiders don't like me practising yoga in the garage—just when I think I have found the perfect venue. I look back at the spider. It hasn't moved.

I continue my practice and finish in head stand, again having an upside down view of the brown spider.

I think I might have to resolve myself to the fact that perhaps I will have to practise with the odd eight-legged visitor, and if I just ignore them, rather than bludgeoning them to death with a plastic water bottle, they might ignore me.

I've had enough spider encounters for one day and will end my practice relaxation in the living room. There's no way I am going to lie down on the mat, with my eyes closed, knowing that the spider is dangling just a couple of feet away from me. I might open my eyes to find the whole garage spider population has come out to sit on the mat. I shudder at the thought.

Feeling slightly paranoid, I roll up my mat and hurry into the living room to a waiting Dave who ravels himself up in the end of the yoga mat while I try to relax. Giving up, I give him the mat and lay on the floor. Despite the spiders, garage yoga is born.

Fourth of July Weekend

I have several choices. To be honest, I can't recall now what they all are but each involves us all going out somewhere to celebrate the Fourth of July. While I want to get into the spirit of things, I can't say I am particularly enthralled at the idea of going somewhere with hundreds of people all packed tightly into a small space to celebrate something that seems like Bonfire Night in summer. I'm not into Bonfire Night all that much in November, but being in America feel I ought to get into the spirit of things and know if I just push myself to go somewhere, I will enjoy it.

I've never really been into going to places where there are great gatherings of people, and in the past few years, have turned into somewhat of a hermit, preferring to stay home and watch a movie. Besides, I know that despite Tom wishing I would make a group decision we stay home, Shelby really wants to go.

'And if you don't put yourself out there, how will you ever meet anyone?' she says now, staring at me rather intently.

Despite having made the decision that 'Mr Right' is definitely here, somewhere in California, just waiting to fall upon my person, I wish perhaps I had kept this intention to myself. I am beginning to feel like something on a shop shelf or for want of a better analogy candy in a candy store!

'Folsom Rodeo,' I declare finally. 'I've never been to a rodeo before, and it will be fun.'

I watch as Tom's eyes do a complete circle in his head.

'Great choice, Grace, just perfect,' he says, rather sarcastically, and then smiles.

Shelby seems pleased.

'There'll be plenty of handsome cowboys,' she says, winking.

The thought of spying handsome cowboys, with my dad sitting right at my heels, doesn't exactly fill me with enthusiasm, but she does have a point.

Not too sure how yoga fits in with cowboys but on thinking about it, I begin to smile as amusing thoughts pass through my head: a yogini and a cowboy! Banish the thought, now what to wear.

It's another scorching hot day and arriving at the rodeo late afternoon will mean being out in the sun in the hottest part of the day. I finally decide on white shorts and one of the new tops I've bought while out shopping with Mum. I'm suddenly obsessed with having no tan lines whatsoever and have gone on a mad buying spree of tops with no straps. The other day Kate said I am fortunate to be able to wear those tops, because she can't, as having such big boobs means they would fall out of them. Poor her! I consider again, looking down at my nearly non existent chest.

The top in question is cute but for some reason squashes my bra and makes me look like I have dented boobs. There's a separate bit of material running down the front of the top, kind of like a frill or scalloped edge as Mum would probably put it, being more materially minded than I am. Frill or scallop, fortunately it's there for one reason, and one reason only, and that's to hide the dented boob on the left side.

Dressed and ready to go, we all pile into the van.

Folsom is such a great place. In the late 1800s, it started out as a small town known as Granite City and home to gold miners wanting to make a fortune in the foothills of the Sierra Nevada Mountains. It reminds me of dream catchers because in Old Folsom, there are lots of shops and many of them carry American Indian gifts. I've visited these shops several times on previous trips to California and have a dream catcher hanging on my bed from one of the very same shops!

Folsom also has some great outlets and so the association of gorgeous Calvin Klein jeans and Saks Fifth Avenue also spring to mind when I think about Folsom. I guess what makes it most famous is the prison, although glad we wouldn't be visiting that!

We arrive at the rodeo in the blistering heat, with dust flying everywhere. Tom's Vanagon seems a little out of place at a rodeo, suited more to surfers and the beach than cowboy hats and horses. Still, we all spill out of the van and wander around, waiting for Mum and Dad to arrive.

There are people everywhere, big trucks, lots of cowboy boots, more hats than a hat store, and yes, indeed, lots of cowboys, most of whom have a cowgirl attached to their arm, I notice.

We soon discover that the rodeo doesn't open until 6.00 p.m. and won't be starting until seven. We catch sight of Mum and Dad making their way to the ticket booth and meet them there to buy our tickets. With a good hour and a half to kill, and with no shade in sight, Shelby sends Tom off to find water. We make our way over to the nearby park and sit on a picnic bench under the trees for shade.

With the temperature over 100 degrees, we are soon feeling the heat. Poor Mum is very inappropriately dressed from head to toe in black, and although the top she is wearing is sleeveless, I am not sure how much use having no sleeves is in this heat.

Very light heartedly I ask why she thought to come to the rodeo with temperatures in excess of 100 degrees all dressed in black. She puffs out a sigh and throws her arms by her side.

'I knew I shouldn't have worn this,' she says, looking down at her top.

'No, no, Mum,' I retract, quickly wishing that I had just kept my gushing forth mouth closed for once.

'It looks great, Mum, it's just boiling hot, and you're wearing black, which attracts the sun.' Can you see the hole I am digging for myself?

'So it looks okay then?' she says, with a worried look on her face.

'Yes, Mum, it really does look great. All I meant was is it's hotter than heck and you'll be hot wearing it.' I am back peddling as fast as I can.

'Well, yes. I realise that now, I think I thought it would cool off later and so wasn't thinking about this earlier heat,' she says her voice softening again.

The trouble with me is that ever since being little, I have always spoken my mind. Mum always used to say to me that I should think before I speak. I literally do speak before I think, and of course, then it's often too late.

A thought of me sitting on a bus when I was little, asking Mum very loudly why the lady sitting opposite us was so fat springs to mind. It's not just what comes out my mouth sometimes either. If I get a thought, I seem to go with it, totally oblivious to the consequences of my actions. Another thought that enough was enough of the constant meanness of my aunt Sandra was followed by me replacing the word 'best' on her birthday card with a very black marker penned 'worst'. I sealed the envelope and sent it off with the other birthday cards for her to open the following day to read in full view of my parents. 'Happy Birthday to the Worst Auntie in the World'.

Tom arrives back to the park with chilled bottles of water, and Leon proceeds to drink most of it at breakneck speed. I have never known a child drink as much as Leon, and I know he is only six but his fish-like drinking does not bode well for when the boy reaches manhood and finds a pub!

We sit around a picnic table and take silly photographs of each other. It isn't difficult because we are all pretty silly really, well except for Dad who says he's not in the mood today to be silly. We decide and tell him that he is probably in the early stages of heat stroke and continue to be silly around him.

Tom takes the kids off to spin on the roundabout, yes, in the 100 degree heat, and we sit drinking the rest of the water before Leon returns to finish it off.

The rodeo preparations are now well under way, and we can see stalls are being set up around the arena to the side of us. We can smell the kettle corn and other delicious aromas, which, being a vegetarian, are no doubt coming from meat products!

Six p.m. finally arrives, and we join the other hundreds of people in line to get into the rodeo. At this point, Tom announces he has actually lost his ticket. It isn't like he is going to find it either; the place is full of people, and he has been back to the van, gone to the store for water, and ran back across to us on the park. He says he wants to buy two tickets anyway and resigns himself to having to spend a small fortune on just getting into the rodeo.

Dad insists the line next to us is going faster than ours, and Shelby, having about a millimetre of patience where Dad is concerned, soon invites him to join it.

After a quick bag search, we finally enter the rodeo and head for the stands to find our seats. It quickly becomes apparent we are going to be like chocolate in a melting pot. It seems even hotter inside the rodeo, and I begin to question my decision-making ability quickly texting Kate that I think I have made a very big mistake and that we are all going to die on the Fourth July from heat stroke. Karma is definitely at work here, and I am beginning to regret having joked about Dad suffering from heat stroke earlier!

After moving around stall D at least four times, we finally settle on the front row having a good view of the rodeo below us. Mum and Tom go off in search of food for everyone and soon return with hotdogs and fries for the kids. I'm sure that Vanessa will soon resemble a hotdog, because at every opportunity since arriving she has ordered one.

Shelby nudges me and says I need to put out some vibes. She says the fact I have an English accent will help my quest enormously. It's just too embarrassing what am I supposed to do: stand up and yell, 'Hey, I'm single and want a cowboy, oh and I speak with an English accent, so come get me!' No, I don't think so.

Each time a remotely handsome looking cowboy strolls by, I can feel Shelby's eyes piercing into my soul.

'You've got to look up, Grace,' she whispers. 'How are they ever going to see you if you don't look up and give out some vibes?'

I am way out of practice, and besides, every time I have ever met anyone before in my life, I had usually been drinking, and so meeting people was easy. After being single for so long and devoting most of my time and energy to yoga, meeting someone is going to be a lot harder than I first thought. I had figured that he would just find me and to be honest, I think I like that idea better. Him finding me will also save all this putting myself out there, staring at people, and vibe giving.

What is really embarrassing is that despite thinking that my dad is actually going a little deaf, he is still sitting right next to me. Giving out vibes to handsome cowboys is not something I want to be doing under his watchful eye!

My thoughts are interrupted by Leon spilling ketchup all over his white trainers.

'Oh, Leon!' I exclaim. 'Why don't you get a napkin?' I say, looking down at his new white trainers, now turning a lovely shade of red.

'I didn't know I was going to spill it, Mum,' he says apologetically.

He is only six, I remind myself, and they will wash. I suddenly realise that we all wear a lot of white. I have just painted the entire inside of my house white and a lot of things in my life are white. My thoughts wander for a moment as I consider why everything in my life is so white.

'Grace!' It's Shelby again. 'Look!' she exclaims.

At that moment I look up and see probably one of the single, most handsome men I have ever seen in my life. Donned in gorgeous blue jeans, a white shirt, and a black cowboy hat, I am in cowboy heaven! I blush, turn away, and hope he hasn't seen me looking like a drooling idiot.

'Go after him!' Shelby orders.

'Oh yeah, right. I can't just chase after some gorgeous man I just saw in the hope that he too is single, realises I am single and speak with an English accent, and finds me irresistibly attractive, no way! And please be quiet because Dad's sitting right next to me!' I plead, hoping that he hasn't heard.

Shelby laughs, obviously finding this far more amusing than I am. 'Grace, you got to get yourself out there. Now where's he gone?'

Her gaze scans the rows below us, but there are just too many people to see where he's gone.

'Back to his gorgeous cowgirl girlfriend, no doubt. Now just stop, please!' I plead again.

The sun fortunately starts to set, and it begins to feel as if we are actually going to cool down rather than die of heat stroke.

Most people have begun to find a seat, and those who haven't are either making their way to one or standing for a short time in front of us.

'Erm, excuse me!' Vanessa says rather too loudly.

'Vanessa!' I exclaim. 'Don't be so rude. People will move, and if they don't, we'll ask them nicely,' I say sternly, as the people standing in front glance up.

Now I wonder where she gets that outspokenness from.

The rodeo announcer booms out that we are going to have a very special guest arriving by parachute.

I am not American and hardly a very patriotic Brit either, but what happens next brings tears to my eyes. If I could pledge my allegiance here and now and become an American citizen, I most definitely would. A guy parachutes out of an aeroplane above the rodeo with an American flag. As he gets closer and closer, we can see that the flag is actually enormous. It's just amazing. We watch as his red, white and blue parachute floats through the air against the azure blue sky and the backdrop of the sun setting. Blaring over the sound system is 'God Bless the USA' by Lee Greenwood.

> And I'm proud to be an American,
> where at least I know I'm free,
> And I won't forget the men who died
> who gave that right to me,
> And I gladly stand up next to you
> and defend her still today,
> 'Cause there ain't no doubt I love this land
> God Bless the USA.

I take some photographs. The American flag he's holding gets bigger and bigger as he heads towards the arena. He lands gracefully in the centre of the rodeo arena where there are people waiting to catch the flag, and they do just that without it even touching the ground. The national anthem rings out and everyone in the stands are on their feet, singing proudly. Despite the heat, goosebumps appear on my arms as the singing gets louder. What a memorable experience, and as we sit down, I look at the photographs I've just taken of the guy parachuting down with the American flag, which are just awesome.

Awesome is a word I use often and since arriving in California, as Tom points out, far too often and far too inappropriately. Tom says that awesome describes massive things, huge events of gigantic proportions, not the things I attach it to. I ask him if this is an appropriate awesome moment but he says not, great maybe, but not awesome. Shelby disagrees with Tom, as she is moved to goosebumps and tears as well. She says that was definitely awesome.

I quickly send a text message to Kate, relaying the whole experience. She is at a family party with Antonio and says she is disappointed not to be sharing the moment with us. I couldn't have gotten this whole Fourth July outing more wrong. I really thought when we first arrived that we were going to be as miserable as sin in the heat and not enjoy it at all. What a great evening it's turning out to be!

The usual rodeo activities then begin with angry bulls and mad bucking horses, and I wonder whether these animals, in fact, enjoy the whole experience of being ridden, roped, and generally ragged about, although on most occasions I have to say they are the ones doing the ragging. Quite rightly so I say, I mean how would you feel having a rope tied around your horns and being dragged to the floor? All in the name of rodeo fun! Shelby assures me that rodeo animals know of no other life and enjoy it. I decide that I will just trust that they do and not let that consume my thoughts and spoil the night.

The interval sees children from the audience descend into the rodeo arena to grab the quarters, cow bells, and other rodeo memorabilia being thrown around by the organisers. I encourage Vanessa and Leon to go join in, but they aren't having any of it. Sam says he is too old for that kind of thing. If twelve is old, then I am history. Dad tries to get them down there too, although I think he secretly wants a cowbell for himself. I tell him he doesn't need the kids and should just get on down there and get one!

Vanessa and I go off to find the toilet. I decide at this point that perhaps cowboys aren't really all that and certainly not the greatest match for a yogini. I mean, despite some of them being incredibly handsome and all gorgeous looking in their jeans, shirts, hats, and boots, most of them are swigging beer from a bottle while carrying at least three more bottles in their other hand. I realise that, in fact, almost all the men around us, whether cowboys or not, are actually doing the same thing.

It's on this trip to the toilet that I also decide to cross cowboys off the list of potential 'Mr Rights'. Yes, I think I have a list going now, didn't before, but I do now and cowboys, or the beer-swigging kind, are definitely off it.

That doesn't mean that harmless flirtation with the one selling cowboy hats isn't allowed though, and as Vanessa and I make our way back to our seats, we are intercepted by one such charming cowboy. Boy probably being the operative word. Hard to say how old he is but definitely younger than me and most definitely somewhere in his twenties. Incredibly nice though and totally smitten with my English accent. Shelby was right after all!

We buy a gorgeous Peter Grimm straw cowboy hat with a brown suede flower on the top that actually looks good on both of us, and we agree to share it. Probably a mistake but seems like a good idea at this time. Vanessa gets to wear it at the rodeo, and she looks super cute.

I think that the gorgeous hat selling cowboy was probably just flirting insanely to get us to buy a hat. Totally fell for that one then, didn't I?

Cowboys still, however, very much off the list.

Tom thinks otherwise, and when we return to our seats and Shelby points out yet another gorgeous bod she has spotted walking by, Tom decides to join in on pointing out hot men.

'Which man, Tom?' I ask, as he quickly points out the passing 'cowboy'.

'There, Grace,' he says pointing at the huge large bellied 'Hells Angel' looking dude walking past us, with long black hair covering most of his head and body.

'Definitely the one for you, Grace,' Tom says finding it hard to stifle his laughter. He then grabs the camera from my hands and snaps a photograph of him.

'So you can keep it and remember him,' he says continuing to laugh.

'Ha, ha, very funny, now stop!' I say beginning to laugh myself.

Shelby is now laughing hysterically at the thought of me and the long-haired 'Adonis' Tom has so kindly pointed out.

The evening ends with a firework display, and I have to say, the best Fourth July I've ever celebrated.

Shelby voices that she wishes Kate had come too so that she could accompany me to the after party, where I could meet yet more cowboys. I am secretly pleased I don't have to go. 'Mr Right' is definitely not a cowboy.

Oyster Mushrooms, Ashtanga, and Tarzan

Kate picks me up late afternoon. I'm looking forward to my second Ashtanga yoga class the following morning, and Shelby has jumped at the chance of looking after Vanessa and Leon while I am gone.

'Not too many sweets today,' I instruct, giving them both a hug.

'Oh, they're fine.' Shelby says, waving her hand dismissively. 'They're on vacation, and besides, when do I ever get to spoil them?'

'Okay, okay,' I relent, 'but not too many.'

'Enjoy your class,' she says, giving me a hug. 'And make sure you take her out tonight,' she says, turning to Kate. 'You never know who you will meet.'

'Right, and before you say it, I know, put out the vibe,' I say laughing.

'See, you're catching on!' Shelby says, pleased with herself.

'Let's go. Bye guys!' Kate says.

I grab my bags, give the kids another hug, telling Vanessa to remember to chill on the sweet intake, and we leave.

We drive straight to San Francisco, somehow missing rush-hour traffic and arrive at Antonio's apartment a little after 6.00 p.m.

'Honey!' Kate shouts, 'Are you home?'

Antonio appears in the doorway of the kitchen. 'Hi, guys,' he says. 'Are we going out to eat? I'm starving!'

Kate kisses Antonio.

'Great idea. We need to take Grace to a restaurant where she can meet cute guys,' Kate says rather blatantly.

'You lot make me laugh,' I cry. 'I feel like I am being served on a plate!'

'I'm under strict instructions from Shelby,' Kate retorts.

'Let's just go out, eat, and have a nice time,' I suggest. 'All this putting me on a plate and getting me out there is putting me off the whole thing!' I protest.

'It's for your own good,' Kate says, pretending to sound stern. 'Tell her, Antonio,' Kate says, looking over at Antonio for him to back her up.

'See, I've been here a week, and she's already got you in on it now, too!'

Antonio laughs. 'Women!' he says.

'Hi, Henry,' I say, bending down to fuss Henry. 'At least, you can't speak and gang up on me.' I stroke him some more and kiss the top of his head.

Henry barks.

'Oh great, so you're in on it too?'

He barks again.

'Total conspiracy,' Kate says, laughing.

Kate and I get changed, and we leave.

Antonio says he's heard of a vegan restaurant that's raved about, and as I'm vegetarian, I might like it. I'm not so sure because I love dairy, especially cheese, and my only experience of anything vegan was a woman, who used to attend a yoga class I went to. She was a complete Earth Mother and often passed wind very loudly in my direction in all the yoga classes. She always arrived late, and even if there wasn't really a space next to me, she would somehow squeeze herself into one. After a Christmas yoga party, where everyone was invited to bring food, I asked her what she had brought, and she introduced me to her vegan curry. Totally explained the wind passing and was basically made up of beans, lentils, and other indescribable mush: things that would only barely pass as food. She offered me a bowl, and for fear of being terribly rude, I accepted. Left too long of an impression on me, and let's just say I was delighted not to have to do yoga after the lunch. So my experience of vegan food to this point wasn't great. However, this was California, and everything I have eaten since getting here has been nothing short of totally delicious.

We start walking up the hill from Antonio's apartment.

'Gosh, I can't believe how warm it is. This is a pretty steep hill,' I say, trying to catch my breath. 'And I thought I was fit!'

'We've been doing some city hikes the past few weekends, so we are getting used to it now,' Kate says, striding ahead.

We reach the brow of the hill and Alamo Square Park offering us a great view of the city and the Golden Gate Bridge, which we can just glimpse through the large Cypress trees. Opposite the park sits the famous Painted Ladies, a row of beautiful Victorian houses which are apparently painted in three or more colours to highlight their architectural features. The houses stand out proudly against the blue sky. We stand in the park for a while, enjoying the views and being surrounded by the magnificent trees.

'Come on then, girls,' Antonio urges. 'I'm starving.'

'The way to Antonio's heart is definitely through his stomach,' Kate says, laughing.

Fortunately, our walk is now downhill and after crossing a few roads, all of which Kate and I run across while Antonio saunters, we have the restaurant in sight.

Antonio thinks it's hilarious that whenever Kate crosses a road, she always hurries or usually runs.

'In England you have to run. Pedestrians don't have right of way like they do over here,' Kate explains to Antonio again. 'Besides, you take it to the opposite extreme, walking as slowly as you can.'

'Just kicking back,' Antonio responds.

'In the middle of the road!' Kate exclaims.

She's right. Just a week before we left for California, I ran across a road in the village near where we live, only to have some lunatic race off at the lights. Missed me by inches! Over here you only have to step off the kerb and cars will stop. In England, you would be arrested for kerb crawling, probably why the cars don't stop for anyone!

We enter the restaurant and wait to be seated. It's small, with the bar and kitchen to the right, and the tables to the left. The room's quite long though and we are seated towards the back where we can see an outside patio offering 'al fresco' dining.

The tables towards the back of the restaurant are high, and we sit on tall barstool type chairs, which Kate falls off as she tries to get on.

Composing herself as the waiter brings over the menus, she then bursts into fits of giggles joking that she hasn't even had a glass of wine yet.

I order a chargrilled vegetable burger while Antonio and Kate order two different Thai dishes.

'Are you excited about tomorrow's class?' Kate says.

'Can't wait!' I say, excitedly.

'So Kate tells me you like this guy,' Antonio says.

'He's just so handsome, and an Ashtanga yoga master, has the dreamiest blue eyes I have ever seen, and am sure a soul to match,' I say, remembering the first time I saw Michael Harvey. 'But he is also married and therefore, off the list completely.'

'Moving on!' Kate exclaims, making us all laugh.

'Moving on, indeed,' I say, agreeing with Kate. 'Seriously though, I feel such an enormous amount of respect for him being my teacher while I am here, and once I start focusing on my practice, I'll forget about how much of a crush I have on him,' I say, trying to convince myself.

'I think it's so cool that you found one of these certified teachers with there being so few of them in the world!' Kate says proudly.

'I know I feel so grateful for that. I just wish he was a bit less gorgeous and not married!' Kate and Antonio laugh.

'Your "Mr Right" is out there somewhere, you know,' Kate says, trying to make me feel better. 'He just hasn't found you yet.'

'Too true!' I say hopefully.

The waiter appears with our meals.

Kate's looks like seafood in rice noodles.

'That can't be seafood,' I say, taking a closer look at the food on Kate's plate.

Kate screws up her nose. 'Ewww.'

'It looks gross to me, what is it?' I say, leaning closer.

'I have no idea, but I am so glad I don't have it,' Antonio says, picking up his fork to eat his own.

Reminding myself that we are in a vegan restaurant, it obviously isn't any kind of animal. However, that still doesn't explain what the half a dozen off white unidentified slimy looking objects are swimming around in the noodles and sauce looking suspiciously like seafood.

'Maybe you should just taste one,' Antonio suggests.

'Knock yourself out!' Kate cries, stabbing one with a fork before offering it to him.

'I think I'll pass on that one,' Antonio says quickly returning to his meal.

'You?' Kate asks, pointing the fork in my direction.

'My vegetable burger looks divine. Thank you,' I say, picking it up and taking a bite.

'Honey, why don't you just ask the waiter?' Antonio says.

Without giving Kate a chance to think about it, I call him over.

'Is everything okay?' he asks.

'Great, thank you,' Kate replies politely. 'We just wondered what these were,' she says, holding up the fork.

The waiter gives us a knowing smile, obviously not the first time he has been asked this question. 'Mushrooms,' he announces.

'Mushrooms!' we all cry in unison.

'Strangest mushrooms I ever saw,' I say, hardly believing him.

'They're oyster mushrooms,' the waiter says, offering more information.

'That totally explains why we thought they were seafood then,' Kate says.

The waiter laughs. 'They do taste good though, enjoy,' he says, leaving the table.

'Yeah, right,' Kate says. 'As if the explanation makes any difference to me wanting to eat one.'

They do look pretty disgusting and wisely Kate decides to eat the noodles and share Antonio's meal instead.

'Well, that was an experience,' I say, as we come out of the restaurant.

'Indeed!' Kate exclaims. 'Vegan food will go down as one of those "been there, done that, and have the T-shirt that doesn't need wearing again" kind of experiences.' We all laugh and run across the street.

The next morning Kate and I get up early, and she drives me to the yoga shala.

'So, just call me when you are done. We won't be far away,' Kate says, as I get out of the car.

'Okay, wish me luck,' I say feeling nervous.

'Luck? You don't need luck. Stop being so nervous, and you'll be fine,' she says and gets out of the car to give me a hug.

I push the buzzer at the door and wait. A girl walks up the street, stops beside me, and punches the numbers to open the door.

Michael is sitting, talking to someone as I walk in. He looks up and smiles.

'Morning,' I say smiling back and trying not to appear like I am shaking from head to toe. I really have to get a grip.

I drop my money into the jar and walk through to the practice room.

Several people have already set up their mats and are beginning their practice. I think I'll wait for Michael to come in and bumble my way through the opening prayer again.

Perhaps I should just recite the Lord's Prayer and be done with it. At least I know that off by heart now.

Dressed once again in blue sweats and a plain white T-shirt, Michael walks through the room and takes his place at the front of the class. With his hands in prayer, he bows his head and begins to chant the opening prayer.

'Vande gurunam, caranaravinde,' he recites.

I repeat it, totally astounded at having understood the first line enough to repeat it!

'Sandarsita . . .' he continues.

After the first word I am totally lost and can't help thinking that it sounded like he said 'san-dar-shit'. No, that can't be right. The opening prayer would not include the word 'shit', surely not.

I try to listen again but am now totally lost and so bow my head a little further and manage to just repeat the last few syllables before chanting *om*, which fortunately you can't go too far wrong with.

I begin my sun salutations. As I am just jumping to my right to start one of the standing series postures, I can't help but notice the man who has just entered the room, in his underpants! Well, they aren't exactly 'Speedo' style, but they are definitely very short, hugging, trunk-style underpants and definitely underwear!

I continue with the posture, praying that he won't stand near me.

Please make him go to the other end of the room, please God, I plead. God obviously isn't listening to me this morning, because the scantily clad man takes his place directly opposite me. I try not to look, but his tight-fitting underpants, which only just cover the top of his muscular thighs, are just begging to be looked at.

I stand back up and, fortunately, for the next posture I have to turn in the opposite direction. After coming back up, I look back across.

'Morning,' he says quietly, before bowing his head to begin chanting his opening prayer. At least he knows the prayer!

He has an American accent but looks more like he would be at home in the jungle. A real-life Tarzan, only with underpants instead of a loin cloth. He's tall, and his body, lean, very muscular, and toned.

I can't say I am immediately attracted to him, but I can't say I'm not either. After all, up to this point, I've hardly looked properly at his face, drawn instead to the tight-fitting underpants. I have to say this does put me off him a little bit, despite the fact that God has obviously blessed him so very well.

Oh my goodness! What am I doing? Shelby has turned me into a crazed, lustful, vibe-giving single woman, attracted to any man that moves.

I shake my head, take a deep breath in, and return my focus to my practice.

Michael comes over and adjusts my posture.

'Thanks,' I say, trying not to look at him. Feeling all hot and bothered about 'underpants man' is difficult enough without staring into the sparkly eyes of a married man!

He stands next to me and continues to adjust and deepen my postures.

'Don't think I am picking on you,' he says softly. 'I just know you are only here for a few weeks and so I want to help you as much as I can.'

'Thanks,' I say, wondering if he is always this nice and whether I can say anything other than thanks, followed by a silly grin.

By the time I reach the sitting postures, I am sweating so much and so engrossed in my practice that I forget all about Tarzan practising next to me. Well, that is until I enter the headstand and happen to glance to my left. It's hard to look at his face, so I once again make eye contact with his underpants and then topple to the right and fall out of my headstand into an unattractive heap on the floor.

Michael appears at my side.

'Are you okay?' he asks, concerned.

I feel ridiculous.

'Fine, thanks,' I say, brushing the hair away from my face and trying to sound very cool about having just fallen into the wall. 'Just lost my balance.'

'Want to try again?' he says encouragingly.

'Sure,' I say, feeling totally embarrassed and wondering whether I can manage to stand on my head without gazing over in Tarzan's direction or at Michael, who is now kneeling right next to me.

Michael explains that the second part of the headstand involves bringing the legs down parallel with the floor and holding before returning the feet to the floor. He further explains that this is much more easily achieved and balance maintained if you stick your bum as far out in the opposite direction as you can.

Fortunately for me, and thanks to yoga, my bum is not the size of Jupiter. However, I am still not at all comfortable with having to stick my bum anywhere near Michael Harvey and feel terribly embarrassed at the mere mention of it. I really do need to get a grip on this crush before the next session.

After holding the headstand for the usual twenty-five seconds, I manage to lower my legs parallel to the floor and, as instructed, stick my bum out to keep my balance, holding for a further ten seconds.

The joy of having achieved this second part of the headstand posture far supersedes anything else I am feeling, and I go into the relaxation room, feeling completely exhilarated.

Just as I am lying down my mat, Tarzan appears. He is now covered in sweat which accentuates his toned body even further.

Get a grip! I tell myself. I must be hormonal. Yes, that's definitely it, hormonal. I think, trying not to look at him.

He smiles. 'You're good,' he says in his sexy deep American accent, unrolling his mat.

'Thanks,' I say, returning his smile. Thanks! Is that all I can ever say? I really need help, I think as I lay down.

I turn my head towards him.

'So are you,' I say. Like I have really seen that much of his practice to comment, I have spent over an hour, trying not to look in his direction, and the few times I have, my gaze seems fixed on his underpants!

I close my eyes and take some deep breaths, somehow needing them now more than ever.

I manage to focus on my breathing and let my mind drift for a while before sitting back up. I roll up my mat and wave at Michael before leaving.

I head back through to the reception room and sit down feeling tired but energised. I call Kate to let her know I have finished.

'Hi,' says Tarzan again, and I really need to stop calling him Tarzan, or 'underpants man,' for that matter. 'I'm Christian,' he says, offering his hand.

'Grace,' I shake his hand. My dad always says that if someone offers you their hand, you should shake it firmly and preferably squeeze it as you shake it. He says this tells other people you are of strong character, and they won't mess with you. He says that you can always tell a person by their handshake, well, that and the state of their shoes. With little time to think, I decide that firmly is quite enough and opt not to squeeze it. He might get the wrong idea.

'Nice name. Where are you from?' he asks.

'England,' I reply. 'You?'

'New York, but I'm in San Francisco, working.'

'Sounds like you have a great job,' I say, impressed.

'I guess. I'm a photographer, so it's more my passion than it is my job,' he says. 'How about you?'

'Well, I live and work in England, but I'm here for the summer, visiting my family who live a couple of hours away from here.'

The fact that he practises yoga in his underpants doesn't seem so much of an issue any more. He actually seems like a nice guy, and because he is dressed now, I am looking at his face long enough to see that he is actually really handsome.

A car horn sounds outside, interrupting my thoughts.

'That'll be my sister,' I say, feeling like I want to stay and talk for just a while longer.

'Right, so you have to go?' he enquires, sounding genuinely disappointed that I have to leave.

'I do, but I'm coming again, the week after next, so hopefully I'll see you then,' I say, wondering if I am being too forward.

'I'm leaving at the end of this week.'

The car horn sounds again.

'I have to go. It was nice to meet you,' I say, picking up my things.

'You too, Grace.'

I pause, wanting to say something else but can't. I smile, reach for the door, and head out.

A shame, but 'Mr Right' is definitely not Tarzan!

Morning Campers!

The rest of the week flies by and is taken up with preparations for our long-awaited camping trip.

I manage to practise yoga before anyone else is awake, well, except for Tom, who's always up before dawn even thinks about waking up. I take a quick shower and set to getting together the last of our things.

Friday, the 10th July and the first day of our eight-day camping trip! We've been waiting for this all year and it's finally here.

I start to sing. If you've ever seen the original Chevy Chase *National Lampoon's Vacation,* you'll know which song I'm talking about when I sing

'I found out long ago,' *(lots of oh oh oh's going on in the background)*

'It's a long way down the holiday road,' (more *oh, oh, oh's*)

'holiday road . . . holiday road.' (This is sung with the word *road* being sung out forever, and then repeated in the same way.)

'Jack be nimble, jack be quick,' (more *oh, oh's*)

'take a ride on the west coast kick.'

Then back to the holiday road chorus again.

I think this song started swimming around in my head part way through yoga. Actually, quite a strange practice: focusing on my breathing and postures while 'Holiday Road' whirs intermittently through my mind. It gave my practice a whole new dimension.

'I have that song whirring around in my head too,' Tom says, walking through the door leading to the garage and launching into song.

'I found out long ago . . . long way down the holiday road.'

I laugh. 'That's so funny because it's been stuck in my head since I got up, I can't believe we have been singing the same song.'

Shelby walks into the kitchen. 'Coffee?' she asks me.

'Yes, please, love some.'

'So, are we packed up?' Shelby says to Tom.

'Just need to grab the last couple of bags and we are good to go,' Tom says.

'Don't forget the pillows,' Shelby says. 'I know you really don't want to take them. Don't be telling me after an hour of driving that you accidentally left them because I won't believe you.'

Shelby has experienced back problems for many years and underwent major back surgery a couple of years ago. As a result, she can't sleep in the tent, but Tom has pimped out the van so that by day it's our main mode of transport and by night Shelby's bedroom suite.

For Shelby, to get a comfortable night's sleep, she needs a few pillows. Tom, on the other hand, has been trying to encourage her to 'rough it' with the rest of us and wants to pack as little as possible.

'I won't forget the pillows. Don't worry and I have even come around to the idea now and packed one for each of us too,' he says, seeming rather pleased for having made that decision.

'Wow! I'm impressed. We're allowed pillows,' I say excitedly.

'You are still only allowed one bag each though,' Tom says. 'Any excess baggage will be removed, and you with it, if there are any objections.'

I laugh. Tom has been telling us all for days that we can only take one bag per person and one carry on. Anything else will be considered excess baggage and therefore not be permitted.

He's been planning this trip for months, and the seating arrangements and things we are taking have all been included in that planning.

'I have birthday presents for Vanessa and me. Am I permitted to take those as additional carry on?' I say, joking.

'We might make an exception, considering it's your birthdays while we are on the trip.' Tom smiles and heads back into the garage to continue packing the van.

Vanessa, Leon, and Sam, who are fast becoming the three musketeers, appear in the kitchen.

'Can we eat pancakes for breakfast this morning?' Vanessa asks, hoping for yet another morning of pancakes and syrup.

'Not this morning, miss,' I reply. 'We are just packing up. Grab yourself a granola bar for now, and we'll stop on the way for an early lunch.'

'A granola bar?' Vanessa says, looking shocked. 'Is that it? I'll be starving.' She furrows up her forehead and purses her lips.

'Then have two, sweetie, but please go with the flow. We need to get going soon. Tom wants us to leave by eight thirty, so we need to eat on the run this morning,' I say, trying to soothe her frustration at not having pancakes.

'I suppose I'll have to then,' she says as though I am forcing her to do something terrible. She joins Leon and Sam, who are already raiding the pantry shelves for breakfast bars.

Shelby packs up the cooler bag with more supplies for the trip, and I fill the cooler with water and cold drinks for everyone.

We pack the rest of our things and go out to the van.

The van really does look great with the new interior, carpet, and covers for the seats. The custom cabinetry Tom has built houses a DVD player and PlayStation. The rear-facing jump seat is to be my new throne for the next eight days. Shelby is going to ride up front with Tom, and the three kids will sit along the back seat, with me facing them.

Vanessa, Leon, and Sam jump in the back of the van and begin scrambling through the cupboards to find headphones.

'Let's get the PlayStation working,' Leon says excitedly.

'Hang on there, you lot,' Tom shouts from the back. 'You'll zap the power if you hook it all up now. Let's wait until we are on the road.'

'Why don't you three go get the cooler bag and the other things from the kitchen and then we'll take some photos?' I suggest.

With everything packed up, we take some photos of us all in front of the van, ready to leave; the 'Holiday Road' song is still whirring crazily around in my head.

The first leg of our trip takes us to Santa Cruz, but we make a stop off at the Mystery Spot, which I am really excited about because despite visiting California many times before, I've never been there. Shelby and Tom buy the tickets, and we have a fifteen-minute wait for our tour to begin.

Other than knowing weird things occur while you're standing in the Mystery Spot, I have no idea really what to expect.

We pull into the parking lot and behind the entrance is steep forest. Our tour guide begins by telling us how the Mystery Spot was discovered in 1939 and defies the laws of physics and gravity.

There are about twenty people in our tour group, and for some reason, the nine strong Chinese family decide that the tour is all about them. We walk up quite steeply into the foot of the forest. As we are guided through different buildings, areas and exercises, we are given the opportunity to try standing in various spots ourselves. It's a weird experience and nothing makes sense, which I guess is the idea! If the floor appears level then you're standing completely leaning forward or backwards. If you feel you are level, then the floor or building isn't. Everyone is eager to take photographs, and the Chinese family, who are reluctant to allow room for anyone to move, appear in most of ours!

After spending far too long in the gift shop, we manage to prise Vanessa, Sam, and Leon away from the souvenirs and head back to the van to continue on our journey to Santa Cruz.

We arrive here midafternoon. It's hot. We aren't really prepared for the beach, with all our swimming things being in bags that are tightly packed onto the roof rack. Fortunately, we have the beach mats, umbrella, chairs, and towels in the back of the van. We decide to just leave unpacking the bags for bathing suits and head to the beach in our shorts.

It feels good to be in Santa Cruz. The last time I was here was twenty years ago. I actually need to double think that because I can't believe it was that long ago. I was just sixteen and spent the day there with Kate and the best friend I made while visiting California that summer.

It looks just the same. I close my eyes and breathe in the warm sunshine, sounds, and smell of popcorn and hotdogs as we walk onto the boardwalk.

Shelby leaves with Sam to find a bathroom, and Tom, Vanessa, Leon, and I walk down onto the beach.

I take my flip flops off at the steps so that I can feel the sand on my feet.

I scream. 'It's boiling!' I yell, quickly jumping back onto the steps and putting my flip-flops back on.

'Guys, keep your flip-flops on while we walk down to the sea, or you'll have no skin left on your feet,' I warn Vanessa and Leon.

It's a great beach with white sand as far as the eye can see. Nothing is more beautiful than being by the ocean, with the sunshine beaming down on you.

'Perfect,' I say to Tom, as I stop and put down the beach mats and towels I am carrying. 'It couldn't get much better than this.'

'Get used to it, Grace. This trip is all about the ocean, and you are going to see a lot more of it,' Tom says.

I love the ocean, and as we will be travelling down the coastal highway, we are going to be by the ocean most of the time. We are planning to head inland to visit Disneyland® where we will be immersed in a little luxury, staying at the Disneyland® Hotel for a couple of nights over our birthdays towards the end of the week and then going into forest for the last stop. Other than that, we'll be right by the ocean.

Vanessa and Leon drop the things they are carrying and race down to the sea.

'Remember, you have to wear those clothes for the rest of the afternoon,' I shout after them.

Shelby and Sam join us, and Tom puts up a chair for Shelby and the umbrella for Sam.

'I hope we aren't going to be by the beach every day,' Sam says crossly.

Sam doesn't like the beach at all and gets no enjoyment from lying in the sun.

'Now come on, we've only just got here,' Tom says. 'Go and play down by the sea with Vanessa and Leon. It's cooler by the water.'

'Oh, all right then, if I have to,' Sam says, looking grumpy as he heads off towards the sea.

Within a few minutes, however, he's enjoying the sand and surf with Vanessa and Leon, all thoughts of disliking the beach and the sun forgotten.

'Keep your eyes pealed then, Grace,' Shelby says.

'Pealed for what?' I say, knowing exactly what she is talking about but trying to sound clueless.

'For a Santa Cruz surfer,' she says.

'Here we go,' Tom says. 'You're in trouble now, you know. Once she gets her teeth into something, she just won't let go.' He laughs.

'I'm just trying to encourage her to put herself out there,' Shelby says, justifying herself.

'I know you are, and I appreciate it, but I think I'll be fine just as I am,' I say, feeling a little embarrassed.

'Well, it doesn't hurt to keep the vibe up. No one will notice you if you don't look,' Shelby says.

'Okay. I promise to look but discreetly please!'

At that moment, Vanessa runs up from the sea, soaked from head to toe.

'A wave just got me,' she says breathlessly as water drips down from her plaits. Her yellow dress, now waterlogged, is a few inches longer, and her shorts underneath are soaked through.

'Well, there goes that outfit for the day then. Don't worry about it now, but I have no more clothes until we get back to the van,' I say.

'Okay,' she says, shrugging her shoulders, racing back to the sea, pleased that it doesn't matter.

I need to lighten up a bit on my usual wanting everything to stay clean and just so. I need to take a leaf out of my yoga book and let things go. We are after all on holiday, and camping, which is going to make a huge difference to how clean things remain. Actually a massive difference as I am sure I am about to find out.

We spend a couple of hours, enjoying the beach and make our way back to the van with a dripping wet Vanessa and Leon. We attempt to de-sand them in the foot shower at the top of the steps from the beach, but they are still pretty much covered from head to toe in sand, so we give up.

'Get used to it, Grace,' Tom says. 'This is just the beginning.' He starts laughing.

'You're enjoying this, aren't you? I am trying to become at one with a little mess here and there.'

We walk back to the van.

'I need the toilet, Mum,' Vanessa announces, as we arrive back at the van.

'Oh, Vanessa!' I cry. 'It's a good ten minutes back to the boardwalk,' I say, frowning at her.

'Sorry, Mum, but I didn't need to go then, but seriously I do now,' she says, crossing her legs.

'Okay, well, let's just go find a bush or something,' I suggest, and we walk off towards the edge of the car park where I can see some trees.

We find a semi-secluded section of bushes behind some isolated cars and do a quick sweep to check there's no one around.

'Be quick,' I say, as Vanessa walks over to the bushes.

I look around us again to check no one is coming and then back at Vanessa.

I can't quite believe my eyes. There she is, standing with her legs spread wide apart peeing like a man!

'Vanessa!' I exclaim. 'I thought you were going to squat down.'

'No, Mum. It's far easier to pee standing up, you know, just like Leon does,' she says, far too calmly.

'I know how Leon pees Vanessa, but you're a girl and girls don't pee standing up. I'm surprised it's not running all down your legs,' I say, now trying to hide my smile.

'Well, art's not the only thing I am good at then,' Vanessa says, giggling.

'So it would seem,' I say, still shocked that she is able to pee standing up. 'Not a talent you want to tell everyone about, though.'

Our first night is to be spent in Santa Cruz KOA, a well-equipped campground with lots of amenities.

We arrive into the parking lot, and Tom goes into the reception to check in and get directions to our camp spot.

'Bad news, Shelby,' he says, as he gets back into the van. 'The way the campsites are set up means that the van has to be parked away from the tent.'

'Great,' Shelby says sadly, looking dismayed. 'How far?'

'Not sure exactly, but let's not get ahead of ourselves and just go find out first,' Tom suggests starting up the van.

The campground is pretty busy. There are RVs, caravans, trailers, and even log cabins.

We drive further into the camp and to where the tents are pitched.

'This is it,' Tom says, as we pull up in front of a paddock-style fence.

In front of us is a large grassy area surrounded by bushes and trees. Lots of tents are already pitched, and there's a shower block to the left.

'Just there,' Tom says, pointing towards the back where there's a vacant spot.

'It's not actually far, is it?' Tom says, turning to Shelby.

Our camp spot is no more than twenty yards in front of the paddock fence.

Shelby agrees. 'No, this is great, Tom. I was really worrying that I would just be isolated in the van, but I'm not too far away at all,' she says, relieved.

'The other campsites we are staying at will be more isolated and so you can park the van by the side of the tent,' Tom says.

'Let's get the tent up before it gets dark,' Tom says, climbing the ladder at the back of the van.

It takes us an hour to put up the tent.

Tom assures me it's a five-man tent. On the plus side, I figure we won't get cold being so snug.

We erect the material partition and decide that boys will go one side and girls the other. I'm not sure whether the five-man tent includes baggage allowance, but suffice to say the bags are at our feet and our heads making us snugger. We are cocooned by a wall of holdalls in a five-man tent.

I soon realise that there is a lot more to camping than I first thought. The most sudden realisation is that I have to live out of this one holdall for the next eight days. The second realisation is that the white trainers I've bought for myself, Vanessa, and Leon are not going to stay white for very long. It isn't that it's muddy, just dusty dry dirt, leaving a greyish film on everything that dares to be white. In fact, most of what I own is white!

Tom is now attempting to put the curtains on the van. Yes, I did say curtains.

Shelby suggested putting the curtains inside the van, but Tom decided he had a better idea and so, in his usual intelligent creative way, he has fashioned, with the help of Mum's sewing skills, some cream canvas curtains that are going to be held in place by steel rods and clips on the outside of the van. What a picture indeed, but they are a perfect fit and something you will probably never see again no matter how many campsites you visit!

As the light begins to fade and the temperature drops a little, we wrap up and light a fire. Our first night camping. Despite the dirt and living out of a holdall, it feels great to be outside under the stars.

Shelby fetches the cooler bags, and we prepare for S'mores, the absolute best sweet outdoor culinary creation ever, and if you have never tried them, then pay attention because you must.

To this point, my only knowledge of S'mores has been them being eaten around the campfire in the movie *Cheaper by the Dozen 2*. However, up to this point, I didn't really know what they were or that they taste as unbelievably good as they do.

Shelby gives each of us a metal skewer with a marshmallow on the end of it. We start to toast them on the fire. The trick is to get your marshmallow to reach a point where it's melting but not exploding and browning but not blackening. At the point it becomes golden brown and puffy, Shelby squishes it between two Graham Crackers and a slab of Hershey's® chocolate. With the heat of the marshmallow, the chocolate begins to melt and there you have it; this is one of the most delicious combinations I have ever experienced.

My first S'more—heavenly! Well, I've had about three actually.

It's now pitch-black, and we decide to get to bed ready for an early start in the morning. Tom tucks Shelby up in the van, locks it, and clips all the curtains shut before heading back to the tent.

We're like sardines in a tin, but it feels cosy and warm, and I'm relieved that I'm not sleeping in a van by myself.

We have a last-minute change of plan and ditch the partition, deciding that as Sam, who I have no doubt will go way beyond six feet when fully grown, is the size of Vanessa and Leon put together, it will work better spacewise if Leon sleeps with me and Vanessa, leaving Tom and Sam on the other side of the tent.

'Move over a bit more, Leon,' I say, feeling I need a little more room.

It makes sense for Leon, being the smallest, to be under the angle of the tent.

'Move further under the eaves,' I say to Leon, pushing him towards the edge of the tent.

Tom starts laughing. 'See, home away from home. Our tent has eaves.'

Leon and Vanessa soon fall asleep, and I can feel myself drifting off.

I jump as I hear what sounds like a man sobbing. Yes, you read that right, sobbing. And I am not talking just a muffled sob here but a really loud wailing kind of sob. It takes me several minutes to actually realise that it's a man because his voice sounds so high-pitched. Here we are in the middle of a campground, in the dead of night, with a wailing, sobbing man; what's going on?

I fumble around for my phone and check the time—ten minutes after midnight. The wailing continues, and it's becoming louder with every sorry sob.

Perhaps he's drunk, I think, trying to figure out what would make a grown man sob.

'Tom,' I whisper, 'are you awake?'

'How can I not be? I was just drifting off to sleep when Bob Marley and his wailer jumped me out of my slumber,' he says.

'What's wrong with him?' I ask, trying not to disturb the kids between us.

'No clue, but he obviously has some issues. Let's just hope he resolves them and goes to sleep!'

However, the wailing continues on, in the same monotonous screeching tone as before.

Surely he must be deranged, but then I wonder whether the worst is yet to come. I check my phone again, twelve forty-five. Thirty-five minutes has passed since he began.

'How much more wailing can he do for goodness sake,' I say to Tom, feeling like we are going to spend our first night camping wide awake.

'I don't know, but surely everyone else in the camp must be awake by now,' Tom says.

'Would you just shut up, man!' We hear someone yell outside at the top of their voice.

The wailing continues, louder than ever.

'What's the problem?' A man's deep voice interrupts the wailing and for one blissful moment, there's once again complete silence.

But a few seconds later, the wailing resumes, and we hear muffled voices. Presumably someone closer to the wailing man has decided that enough is enough, either that or the police have been called to cart him away for disturbing the peace.

The wailing stops. I check the time; 1.00 a.m.!

'Night, Tom,' I whisper.

'Finally!' Tom replies. 'See you in a few hours,' he says, shuffling in his sleeping bag.

I push Leon further under the eaves to get some space and close my eyes, welcoming the beautiful silence.

A Concrete Ship, Castroville, and Monterey Beach

I quickly realise that perhaps just packing shorts, vest tops, and flip-flops isn't such a great idea when you are going to be by the coast. Tom pre-warned us that it might be a little chillier in the mornings and evenings, so I packed a couple of jogging bottoms for each of us and one or two sweatshirts.

I often say it and will say it again; hindsight is such a beautiful thing. We are full on camping, and from here on in there will be no real amenities. Showers maybe, but certainly no laundry facilities, and the few warmer clothes we have are soon going to get pretty dirty.

We say our goodbyes to the KOA campsite and the wailing man, whoever he is. Our next destination is Seacliff State Beach, to see, of all things, a concrete ship. I know, I've been thinking the same thing, how can a concrete ship float? But it has done for a very long time and still does.

I am sure the sun wants to make an appearance but is just hiding behind all the clouds. Every now and then it seems to get lighter, as though it's just breaking through, only to be covered over again by clouds.

I love the sun and in the week leading up to the camping trip, when we've been 'home' at Toms, I've spent most days out by the pool. I am, however, careful and wear Vanessa and Leon's high factor sunscreen. I want a great tan by the time I go home but gone are the days when I'll slap on the oil to sizzle.

We make our way down to the beach and towards the ship. As we walk along the pier, it becomes apparent that the ship has obviously been here for a very, very long time indeed. It's covered, and I mean covered, in birds, mostly seagulls and the odd seal here and there. To say that there's a lot of bird poo is an understatement. I'm talking years and years of bird poo. Crap ship is a better description than concrete ship.

Tom, as always, knows the answers to most questions, and if he doesn't, he still has a good answer anyway. It's just the way he is.

The concrete ship is S. S. Palo Alto. It was built by the San Francisco shipping company at the end of World War I and launched in May 1919.

In 1929 the ship was bought by the Seacliff Amusement Corporation who towed it to Seacliff State Beach. A pier was built leading out to where the ship was rested on the ocean floor. It was then refitted as an amusement ship to include a dance floor, swimming pool, and cafe. Sadly, two years later, the corporation went bankrupt, and the middle section of the ship cracked. All the fittings that had been added two years previously were taken off the ship, and it was left to be used as a fishing pier. Over time, the ship became unsafe and was closed off with iron gates, preventing anyone access.

Several fishermen are already set up for the day as we arrive at the end of the pier.

The ship has sat in this very spot for eighty years. Twisted steel that once reinforced the ship pokes through the concrete, which is cracked and crumbled. It's hard to believe that this was once an amusement ship. As sad and sorry as it looks, it is now home for lots of marine life and is going to end its days as a concrete reef.

Shelby has seen enough of the concrete ship.

'Keep your eye out for joggers,' she says as we start to walk back down the pier.

'Joggers?' I ask. 'What ever for?'

'Clueless!' she says, nudging me. 'Because, you might see some hunky jogger, and knowing you, he will completely pass you by because you are gazing out to sea.'

'But I like the sea.'

'Yes, I know that, silly, but it's not going to bag you "Mr Right," is it?'

'Neither is harassing "9.00 a.m. Seacliff Beach" joggers,' I say, pulling a funny face.

We grab some coffee from the cafe and walk along the beach and, of course, I get everyone doing yoga poses on the sand.

As we walk back towards where the van is parked, large groups of people are setting up a luau.

Tom dares me to run off with a melon, but I decide not to rise to the challenge. I don't want to end up being chased down the beach by thirty strapping Hawaiians, although, on the other hand, I am sure Shelby will consider this a good move.

Tom has planned the trip so that each day will see us in a new place and moving on to camp in a new campsite. This is, as I mentioned, with the exception of our birthdays, which are later in the week. I am going to be turning thirty-seven and the following day Vanessa will celebrate her tenth birthday. What's great about Tom's planning is that our travelling time each day is kept to a minimum.

As we drive away from Seacliff Beach, the skies darken. I am beginning to wonder whether it actually might rain.

'It's California!' I exclaim, thinking out loud.

'Yes, Grace, it is, taken you a whole week to realise that, hasn't it?' Tom says jokingly.

'This is no joking matter, Tom. What I mean is that it's California and why is the sky that colour?' I say, wondering where the 90—and 100-degree weather has disappeared to.

'Coastal weather is very different to the weather we get inland, Grace, and to us this is perfect. We've been living in 100-degree weather for weeks now,' Tom says, seeming quite happy that the temperature is cool and the sky overcast.

'Well, newsflash! We are from England, and we came to California for guaranteed sunshine,' I say, rather sullenly.

Tom starts laughing. 'It burns off later in the day, but it's generally cooler by the coast, anyway. It'll be fine, you'll see. When we get back next week, and you've had a few days melting in the heat again, you'll be wishing for this coastal weather,' he says, trying to reassure me.

Just then rain begins to fall on the windscreen.

'Oh, for the love of God,' I say, not quite believing that it's July in California and it's raining.

'I have my bikini on underneath these shorts and vest!' I exclaim. 'We are going to freeze and get soaked.' I am beginning to feel concerned. Even though we live in England, I am very fair weathered.

'Grace, just chill about the weather. It'll be fine. Do you want me to stop somewhere so you can stock up on sweats?' Tom says, trying to provide a solution.

'Yes, I think I do. That would be a good idea, especially considering we are all wearing shorts!'

We stop at some outlets and find an Old Navy store where I buy Vanessa and Leon some sweats and myself a couple of sweatshirts too.

The rain seems to clear as quickly as it arrived, and I am relieved that we aren't actually in the midst of a complete drowning on our first couple of days camping.

We drive into Castroville just before lunch.

Tom informs us that we're in for a real treat today. Having already visited a concrete ship, we are now going to have the honour of seeing a giant concrete artichoke. I think he might be joking, but Shelby assures me he isn't.

I have, to this point, never heard of Castroville, but Tom, being the grand tour guide that he is, informs us all that Castroville calls itself the 'Artichoke Center of the World'.

I have tasted artichokes once in my life. Remember me mentioning the marine I met when I was younger? Well, I had dinner at his sister's house, and she cooked artichoke, which I then ate by dipping them in mayonnaise and scraping them along my bottom teeth. Not pleasant and not something I want to repeat either. What is it with these weird vegetable experiences? I'm amazed I remain a vegetarian sometimes (or vegetable as Leon sometimes refers to me as).

Tom, who is one of, no correction, *the* fussiest eater I have ever known, would never eat an artichoke. The obvious appeal is the fact that this town has a giant concrete one and concrete is, I am discovering, the theme of the day.

We follow the signs to the concrete artichoke while Tom gives us some more fascinating Castroville facts.

'Each year there is an Artichoke Festival where there is an artichoke parade and a coronation of the Artichoke King and Queen,' he says, wowing us with his knowledge.

'And', he continues, 'in 1948, Marilyn Monroe was crowned the Artichoke Queen.'

I like Marilyn Monroe, so that seems pretty cool really, but still doesn't change my mind about eating artichokes.

'There it is!' cries Vanessa, pointing to the huge green artichoke.

We park up to investigate.

Tom was right: a giant green concrete artichoke stands before us.

There is nothing more to do than take lots of photos of us all posing next to the concrete artichoke and one with Tom climbing up it.

We decide that now is a good time for lunch and head into the deli next door. We all agree that despite there being every imaginable way to eat an artichoke, we'll pass up on the delicacy and opt for something a little more familiar. Fried artichoke just isn't making my mouth water!

The drive to Monterey Beach is beautiful, and as we draw closer, the sun makes frequent appearances as it finally burns its way through the clouds.

'I might actually catch some sun on this beach!' I exclaim, feeling relieved to see the sun.

'Let's hope you catch more than the sun,' Shelby says.

Tom begins to make the sound of the *Jaws* theme. 'Just when you thought it was safe to go back on the beach.' He laughs. 'There she goes again,' he says humorously.

We park the van and unload the beach gear.

Sam, Vanessa, and Leon run ahead. The beach is quiet with a few canoe parties heading out further along the shore.

Although the sky is still a little cloudy, the air feels warm. Probably because it's cooler than it was yesterday at Santa Cruz. Sam seems more enthusiastic about being by the beach and is enjoying playing in the surf with Vanessa and Leon.

Sitting on the beach, I can see seven sailboats on the horizon, and I can just make out the different colours of their sails. I take a great photograph of Sam, Vanessa, and Leon splashing in the sea, with their backs to the camera and the boats as the backdrop against the horizon.

Tom starts to play Frisbee® with Leon but with a rather overzealous first throw, smacks poor Leon right on the side of the eye, almost knocking him out. Shelby suggests that Tom leaves the Frisbee for the time being and leave Leon to enjoy the sea.

At the Old Navy store, earlier, we bought Leon an American football, which he's now enjoying throwing in the sea and retrieving when the tide brings it back to his feet.

Leon also discovers sand angels, which melts Aunt Shelby's heart. This lovely moment is soon, however, interrupted because Leon experiences the downside, having wedged far too much sand in his shorts, causing very uncomfortable chaffing! Tom makes up for almost knocking him out earlier and takes him down to the sea to try and wash some of the sand away.

This trip feels perfect as it is . . . with or without the elusive 'Mr Right'.

Laguna Seca Mazda Raceway Grand Prix Campsite

The campsite at the Laguna Seca racetrack is to be our home for the second night.

We're very excited at the thought of camping by the side of a world-renowned race track where even Steve McQueen himself has raced-well, back in 1959, but it's still very exciting.

Laguna Seca is nestled among the hills overlooking Monterey Bay, and after a short drive, we arrive into the recreation park late afternoon.

We drive alongside the race track as we make our way up a dirt road to find our campsite.

Tom receives a royal 'hip hip hooray' when we realise he has booked us into the number one camp spot, directly overlooking the famous turn 8 and 8a known as the Corkscrew. In motorsports, this is considered to be one of the worlds' most challenging turns!

We thought the views were spectacular on the drive up, but that was nothing compared to this. To the left and front of us is the track and to the right nothing but hills as far as the eye can see.

After the hustle and bustle of the KOA campsite we left this morning, this is heaven. It's just like camping is supposed to be: quiet and peaceful.

Although the sun is still shining, the wind is picking up. By the time Tom manages to get the first of the camping equipment off the van; it's blowing a gale. The van's parked on a dirt site with some steps leading down to a second dirt pitch which is directly above the track.

'Where's the best place to put the tent, Tom?' I say, pulling my hood up over my head and trying to keep myself out of the wind.

'The ground's too hard up here by the van, so let's put it down there,' he shouts, trying to make himself heard above the wind.

It isn't long before we realise just what a mission this is going to be. The wind is howling by this point, and we are struggling to hold the tent down. The ground is too hard to nail in the tent pegs, and so we begin to fill the front of the tents with the biggest rocks we can find.

Sam decides that he isn't going to be whisked off the hillside in the middle of the night and wants to 'jump tent'. He goes off to talk to Shelby about the prospect of him sleeping in the van.

'No way, Sambo. We are in it for the long haul, and if we are blowing off the hillside, then you are coming with us,' Tom shouts up after him.

Sam rejoins the ranks and decides to stick it out. We assure him he will not be falling off the hillside because we have of it in rock form, holding down the tent from the inside.

We think we'll probably need to hole ourselves up for the rest of the evening in either the tent or the van, but as soon as we set up camp, the wind dies down and peace and quiet is once again restored. Perhaps Mother Nature is just having a little fun with us.

The sunset over Laguna Seca raceway is breathtaking. Tom and I take as many photos as is humanly possible with two cameras, little light, and not much technical photographic experience between the pair of us.

With the sun setting, Tom lights a fire, and we decide that S'mores are definitely on the menu. Yes, for a second night running. As an official S'mores ambassador, if you still haven't tasted them, you should go and make some right now, and come back to reading this book when you have tried them.

After an enlightening lesson on which stars are which (how Tom knows all this stuff I will never know), I ask Tom if he'll come to the toilet with me because, well, frankly it's now pitch-black, and the nearest toilets are two portable ones about twenty-five yards away from our camp spot.

We take the lantern and as we walk up, swinging from a tree right in front of us is the biggest spider I have ever seen in my life. I decide to name it a ghost spider, because not only is it a white greyish colour, but with the lantern illuminating the path, its shadow is projected to ten times its size. It's like something out of *Arachnophobia*, only much worse. We give it a wide berth because it's swinging from the tree, and we are a bit concerned about getting tangled up in its web and becoming dinner!

Portable toilets don't need an explanation, do they? But here's a good one: dark, dirty, and well, basically comprising a black hole.

Tom opens the door and holds out the lantern, which barely illuminates the dark space within.

If I thought the white ghoul hanging from the tree was scary, what emerges from the darkness as Tom shines the light into the loo makes us both jump.

Dangling from the toilet roll is a black widow spider! It looks like I am really going to go to the toilet in there.

'Oh my god!' I cry. 'Is that really a black widow spider?'

'Oops, better not go in that one then, Grace,' Tom says with little reaction.

'Aren't you scared?' I say, feeling like there are ten of them crawling down my back.

'No, not really. Just leave it be and it won't hurt you. Go in the next one, Grace,' Tom says, closing the door.

Tom opens the second loo door and shines the lantern.

'There's nothing in here but a black hole,' Tom says.

I stand considering my options. I really need to go, and unless I want to walk down to the toilet block, I don't have much choice.

'It'll be fine, Grace. Just go. No black widow, just a black hole,' Tom says, laughing at his own humour.

'It's okay for you to laugh. You're not the one having to go in there,' I say nervously.

I go through the door.

'I don't think I can do this,' I say. 'You're going to have to stay there, right with the door in your hand, just in case.'

Tom closes the door leaving it slightly open so that I can still see the light. He stands directly in front of the door.

I begin to pee and start laughing.

'I'm really sorry that you have to stand right in full ear shot of your sister peeing,' I say.

We can't stop laughing and then head back to tell Shelby our gruesome tale of spiders. In the process, we also manage to scare the kids half to death, and they are all convinced that they are going to get eaten alive by spiders in the middle of the night.

Dawn breaks, and through the mist, I can make out the sunrise. It's so peaceful, looking across the hills, with the mist rolling in from the ocean beyond them.

I intended to practise yoga, but the wind is whipping again and it's freezing. I say to Tom that I'll go and shower early and then come back for some coffee.

Although there are other people camping, the spots are well spaced out, and it seems we are the only people mad enough to be up and about.

The toilet block is isolated and a good five minutes walk away. Although I am a little nervous about heading down there on my own, I really want to have a shower.

'Do you think I'll be okay, going down there so early?' I ask Tom.

'Yes, Grace, of course, you will. Ring me if you need to. I've got my phone,' he says, looking up as he tries to light the stove in the wind.

I take my bag, grab the mobile phone out of the tent, and head off up the track towards the toilet block. As I reach the brow of the hill, I hear an engine start up. It makes me almost jump out of my skin and as I look over to the left, I see a truck parked. My immediate thought is: why is he parked there without a tent?

The truck pulls off the dirt and slowly begins driving up behind me. I frantically rummage for the phone in my bag and push the call button to Tom.

'Grace?' Tom answers. 'What's up?'

I can't speak fast enough.

'Tom, there's a truck. There's no tent, though, and when I went past, it started up, and he's just drove by me.' I am still walking and can see the toilet blocks in the distance. 'He's just parked outside the toilet block. What shall I do?'

It seems totally bizarre to me that someone would just happen to be starting their truck up at the very moment I walked past and is now going into the toilet block where I am going!

Just then the phone cuts off.

'Tom?' I yell, down the phone, a feeling of dread creeping up on me.

'Tom!' I yell again and then realise the phone battery has died.

'Oh, that's just perfect,' I say out loud.

I look down the hill to where the toilet block is and the blue truck is now parked in front.

It's in one of those situations where you have one 'little me' on one shoulder, which is telling me I am imagining it and to stop being ridiculous and go shower, and the other 'little me' on the other shoulder, telling me that I might never see daylight again if I go down to the shower block.

At that moment Tom appears.

'My battery died,' I say, relieved to see him. 'Do you think I'll be safe going down there by myself, Tom?' I say nervously.

'Grace, lots of people sleep in their trucks, you know. He was probably driving somewhere, thought it was late, and so stopped off overnight and slept in his truck.'

'It scared me to death. I was just walking along and then the truck just started up. I jumped out of my skin.'

'It just made you jump, Grace, that's all. You skin is still intact and it's perfectly okay. You'll be fine,' Tom says.

'Right, thanks Tom. Okay then, I'll go,' I say, convincing myself I am being ridiculous and as Tom said, will be absolutely fine. 'I'll be back soon then.'

'All right, Grace, just ring Shelby's phone if you need me. Here's my phone,' Tom says, handing me his phone before turning and running back in the other direction.

The shower blocks are in one building, with the entrance to the women's side in front. I'm not sure where the entrance to the men's is, but as I walk past the blue truck, I hear a shower running to the left and so I figure the entrance must be to the left side. I hurry through the women's door.

A few things are bothering me. First, I am not convinced that he is just an 'innocent sleeping in the truck overnight en route somewhere man'. It still seems odd that he started his truck up just as I walked by.

Second, there is no way of locking the women's part of the building. It's like a long room, with hand basins to the right as you walk in. The toilets are beyond the basins and then the showers right at the bottom with just curtains across each one. No locks whatsoever. He will hear the shower, come right in, do whatever he feels like doing, and no one will hear my screams because I am right at the end of the building, and there is no one else around. Why did I get it into my head that I'd shower this early and why when I first got freaked out did I not just think I'll come back later and go back to Tom?

Again, back to the 'little me' on one shoulder and the 'little me' on the other. 'Big me' stuck in the middle!

I stand near the entrance and listen to the running shower in the men's block. I can hear metal, like a chain of some kind and that just sends all sorts of thoughts racing through my head.

He's going to chain me up and put me in the back of his truck. 'No, he isn't!' says the reasoning 'little me' on the other shoulder.

I take a deep breath.

'Right!' I say aloud, walking down to the showers.

I put my bag on one of the blocks outside the shower and stand looking into the cubicle.

The shower in the men's block is still running, but whatever the chain noise was, it's now stopped.

I unzip my fleece and then realise that to get in the shower, I have to take all my clothes off. Kind of reminds me of the time when I went into labour with Vanessa and asked the nurse if I needed to take off my underwear.

'No way,' I say to myself, realising how ridiculous it is to be totally naked getting into a shower that has no lock, with goodness knows who's, just a few feet away, waiting to do goodness knows what to me.

I pick up my bag and walk back to the door.

I'll stay here until the truck drives off, and then I'll have a shower. This solution appeases both the 'little me's' on my shoulders. I am acknowledging that perhaps the man next door does have sinister intentions, and I am also acknowledging the fact that it's okay and no need to run back to camp.

I wait a few minutes and hear the shower stop. I wait again. More minutes pass. I can hear footsteps. They are coming from the right!

My heart begins to thump in my chest. Hang on a minute! Why is he coming from the right if the men's shower block is to the left?

Oh my god! Why didn't I go back when I had the chance? Now he's going to get me.

My heart is now pounding so much that I feel like my ears are going to explode.

The footsteps are getting closer.

I flip open Tom's phone and dial the button for Shelby.

She answers.

'Get Tom, I need Tom to come quick,' I whisper frantically.

'Grace?' Shelby asks sleepily. 'Is that you, where's Tom, and where are you?' she asks, totally bewildered.

'Quick, Shelby. I need Tom!'

I hang up and at that very moment the man reaches the door of the women's block.

I hold my breath and look up, my heart beating against my chest.

'Morning,' the man says cheerily as he walks by.

I must look totally horrified.

'M . . . morning,' I stammer the word out as best as I can and then let out a huge sigh as I breathe out.

I hear the truck start up and see Tom running down the hill towards me. I burst into tears.

'Oh, Tom,' I cry. 'I heard this chain noise, and I couldn't get myself to get in the shower, so I waited, and then he came from this way, and I thought he was going to tie me up and put me in his truck,' I say stifling a sob.

Tom gives me a hug.

'It's all right, Grace. Your mind just got a bit carried away,' he says. 'He was walking that way because that's where the entrance to the men's shower block is.'

'But I heard the shower to the left side and so thought that was the entrance round there,' I say.

'No, Grace. The entrance is the other side, but the shower block runs to the back of you, which is why you heard it that side,' Tom explains.

'Right,' I say, still crying and now feeling a bit stupid. 'I am such a div, aren't I? I can't believe I got myself into such a state over someone innocently taking a shower.'

'It's okay, Grace,' Tom says again. 'Your mind does funny things sometimes,' he says, trying to make me feel better.

'This whole camping thing is really new to me, Tom, and now look at me, all emotional and in tears,' I say, sniffing and feeling a bit sorry for myself.

'Well, in that case, you have learnt something new about yourself today then,' Tom says.

'Yes, that I am scared of things that aren't really there,' I say.

'Everyone has things they are scared of, Grace. Don't worry about it too much. Shelby didn't know what was going on. She said she was woken up by the phone, and it was mine, but then you spoke, and she couldn't figure out what was going on.'

We laugh.

'She popped her head out the van window and told me Grace needs you. I had an idea that you had been spooked, so came running down. Are you sure you are going to be okay now?' Tom says.

'Yes, I'll be fine, thanks, Tom.'

This time, I get in the shower and manage to get back to the van, without being harmed by an axe murderer along the way.

Several hours later, with the clouds having cleared, the sun emerges, and as we pack up to leave, we hear the faint sounds of car engines in the distance. Race practice has begun, and we are right in full view of the famous turn to witness some spin-outs as the cars hurtle around the track.

A little to the right of the bend is a watchtower, and shortly after the racing begins, a black car draws up. A guy gets out with coloured flags and makes his way to the top of the tower.

Tom is busy packing the van, and Vanessa, Leon, and Sam are off, playing on the small park that is close by.

'He looks nice, Grace,' Shelby says as I stand watching the racing.

'I hadn't noticed,' I say, not exactly telling the complete truth. Okay, so I had noticed but only because I happened to be standing and watching the racing as he pulled up.

'Why don't you go talk to him?' Shelby encourages.

'I can't talk to him, he's obviously involved in the racing, and I'll distract him. Besides, he's too far away to speak to,' I say, trying to come up with as many excuses as I can think of.

I've never gone up to anyone I don't know and just spoken to them, well, not in this context, anyway. It was always the other way around and people have spoken to me when I was out or at least in a place where you expect to just speak to people you don't know, like in a club or a bar or somewhere. I really am totally out of practice and way out of my comfort zone. Do people actually just speak to random people in the hope of sparking some interest? I wonder.

Shelby interrupts my thoughts.

'I think his name is Josh,' she says, laughing.

'Josh?' I ask, looking totally confused. 'And where did that name pop up from then?'

'He just looks like a Josh,' she says.

We both laugh.

'He'd be a perfect boyfriend, could take you racing for the day, he has a really interesting job.' Shelby PI is on the case again.

'How do you know what his job is? He could just stand and wave flags all day,' I say, looking over at him.

I turn away from the track and collapse the chairs to pass to Tom.

In the meantime, 'Josh' has moved from his lookout tower to another platform that is actually right in front of our camp spot.

He obviously isn't just the flag man because I can hear him talking into his radio, communicating with someone to tell the drivers how to adjust and improve their driving at turn 8.

I walk back towards the chairs, and he looks over.

'Well, it's now or never, and what's the worst thing that can happen?' I ask myself.

'Hi,' I say, trying to sound very laid back.

'Hey, how are you?' he says, turning to look at me.

I smile and then just as I open my mouth to speak . . .

'Hey, good, thanks! How are you?' yells a very loud Tom, from the top of the van.

I turn around to see Tom waving.

'Josh' turns back around, obviously thinking that this is my obsessive boyfriend or, God forbid, husband, yelling back.

I race up behind the van and began to laugh hysterically.

Shelby, having witnessed the whole thing, gives Tom what for.

'Tom, you complete moron. He was talking to Grace. She said "hi" and then you, you great lump, go waving your arm and saying, "hey, good thanks, how are you"!' Shelby mimics Tom's voice.

Tom is clueless.

'Well, I didn't know that. I just heard him say, "hey, how are you," and I assumed he was talking to me, so I responded,' he says.

'Well, how is she ever going to meet someone, with you jumping in there? You have to make sure people know you're with me,' Shelby says.

By this point, we are all laughing our heads off, and it becomes very apparent to me that Laguna Seca is unfortunately not going to be the setting to spark a new romance.

Big Sur and McWay Falls

After leaving Laguna Seca, we decide to find somewhere nice to have breakfast.

Having driven around the same blocks three times, Tom finally relents by stopping, enabling me to ask someone for directions. I know it's stereotyping, but in my experience, men do not like asking for directions. Fortunately, the person I choose to ask is a waitress on her way to work at a restaurant that is due to open any minute. What are the chances?

'You can't get much better than that!' I exclaim, pleased with myself. 'See, it pays to stop and ask directions,' I say to Tom.

'I knew there had to be a restaurant around here somewhere, and we would have found it in the end,' he says, justifying himself for having driven around in circles for the past fifteen minutes.

'Yes, probably around lunch time,' I say. Shelby and I laugh.

After roughing it and living out of a bag for the past few days, the Lalla Grill restaurant is heaven sent. Everywhere is pristine white. As we enter, Tom starts to laugh.

'This is definitely for your benefit, Grace,' he says.

I can't say it enough; I just love white. The whole restaurant was designed using clean lines and white furniture, which are the perfect contrast against the bold bright orange and lime green soft furnishings. There is the most amazing bar at the front of the restaurant, which has boxed shelves filled with bottles and glasses, running floor to ceiling, with a white ladder running across.

I decide this is going to be a delicious experience.

We are shown to our seats by a very handsome waiter; delicious indeed, I think. I might say these things to myself but the actuality of saying them out loud or acting on them is another matter entirely.

'This is definitely for your benefit, Grace,' Shelby says, nudging Tom and pointing in the direction of the waiter.

'I think Grace has had her lesson in flirting for one day, back at the racetrack,' he says.

'She would have had her lesson in flirting if,' she pauses and then says, 'Hey! good thanks, how are you!' Shelby again mimicks Tom's response when 'Josh' had spoken to me, back at the racetrack.

I can't help but laugh about it. Tom had been so oblivious to the fact that 'Josh' was actually speaking to me.

The kids are excited about having Belgian waffles for breakfast and debating on whether to get sausages or bacon to go with them, finally deciding on both.

The waiter returns to the table, smiles at me, and asks me what I would like. I feel embarrassed, feeling my cheeks glow a little, but think what the heck and smile back.

He takes our orders and goes off to fetch coffee.

'He was so into you,' Shelby says.

'He was not. All waiters smile at you, and it's part of their job.'

'He was taking our orders and still smiling at you,' she says, laughing. 'You should speak to him.'

'Oh no, not again, wasn't this morning enough of an embarrassment? Besides what am I supposed to say? Erm, excuse me, but I am from England and would really like to meet "Mr Right" and you look just the part!' Okay, so perhaps a little over the top but seriously, what am I supposed to say?

'No, silly, it's just practice for when you do meet "Mr Right". It doesn't hurt to just practise, and you are clearly so out of practice,' Shelby says.

'Oh thanks!'

'You know what I mean. You haven't dated anyone for years, and this is a great opportunity for you to get back into it.'

'Noted,' I reply curtly. 'But not in the middle of a crowded restaurant, with my children sitting either side of me, eating Belgian waffles. Thank you very much!'

'You don't need a man anyway, Mummy,' Vanessa chips in. 'You are okay as you are,' she says, patting my arm.

'Right!' I exclaim. 'Let's change the subject, shall we? These spoons are amazing,' I say, picking up one of the sugar spoons. 'What an unusual shape, how cool!'

Tom laughs. 'Seriously? In two seconds we have gone from discussing "Mr Right" to the shape of the end of a sugar spoon.'

'Yes, seriously. I love this spoon. I wonder if they will let me take one home, you know, like as a souvenir.'

Shelby laughs. 'Honey, if you ask that guy, he'll let you take anything you want home, including him!'

'Shelby! How terribly rude!' I say in my best prim voice. We laugh as the waiter returns to the table with coffee.

'Excuse me,' I say. 'We are visiting from England, and I know it's silly, but I really love these sugar spoons. Do you think I could have one? I don't mind paying for it.'

The waiter turns, leans towards me, and says that there is no need to buy one. I am most welcome to just take one with me.

'Ha! I told you!' Shelby says.

'He was just being nice,' I say, putting the spoon into my bag and grinning.

'Of course he was, and if I had asked him for a spoon, he would have told me politely that the cutlery was the property of the restaurant and not for sale,' Shelby says.

Breakfast is delicious, and we are all delighted by the fact that the bathrooms are just as exquisite as the restaurant. It feels strange, actually being able to sit on the toilet seat! Oh the simple pleasures in life!

Our next stretch of driving takes us through what's known as Big Sur, the coastal region where the Santa Lucia Mountains meet the Pacific Ocean.

Highway 1 winds alongside some of the most amazing coastal scenery I have ever seen. At times we are high up, driving along the winding highway, with a 100-foot-rugged drop literally being inches away from us, and then at other times, right on the level of the beach and the ocean.

Tom enjoys manoeuvring the van around the winding turns and, much to Shelby's dismay, makes a few sharp swerves on occasions. She's therefore quite relieved when I make Tom stop several times so we can make the most of the scenery and take some photographs.

We are heading for McWay Falls, which is part of Julia Pfeiffer Burns State Park.

The land on which the park now sits used to be known as Saddle Rock Ranch because interestingly, the coastal rocks resemble a saddle.

We park in a redwood grove and make our way rather hastily, I might add, to find the toilets.

After having spent a couple of days on the road, we are now beginning to grade the bathroom facilities along the way, and the art of standing while peeing is becoming bizarrely natural.

I am using antibacterial gel as if it's hand cream and keeping a regular supply of tissues in my bag for every eventuality.

These bathrooms are not the greatest on the trip, I have to say, but I think the smell is more overpowering than the state of the toilets themselves. Obviously, the fact that there is no light in the bathrooms doesn't help. Not only does this hinder Shelby's trip to the toilet, but it is also obvious that she hasn't quite got the hang of standing, peeing like the rest of us have.

'Just look at me,' she exclaims, looking quite disgusted with herself.

She turns around for us to view the large wet patches down the back of her trousers.

'Oh dear,' is all Tom can reply, stifling his giggles.

'I can't believe the state of me,' Shelby continues, taking all the laughter she has created among us quite well.

'Just stay there, and let me get a picture,' Tom says, taking the camera out of his bag.

'Oh sweet Lord! Here I am looking like I peed myself, and my husband is capturing it all on film.' She smiles at Tom.

We burst out laughing again and head off up the trail.

There are lots of trails to choose from, but we have come specifically for the Scenic Trail which takes us from the redwood grove along McWay Creek and through a tunnel that passes underneath Highway 1.

The views when we reach the other side are breathtaking and definitely awesome!

We are about a 100 feet above sea level, and from the trail have panoramic views of the ocean. Below us is the famous McWay Cove, where, from the opposite cliff, the waterfall tumbles eighty feet from the top of the granite cliffs directly into the Pacific Ocean. The cove itself is like something out of the Blue Lagoon: beautiful white sandy beach with turquoise sea.

We take so many photographs that we stop the flow of people walking along the trail.

The cove is pretty inaccessible from above, and so for both safety and environmental reasons, no public access is allowed.

We continue along to the end of the trail to view the remaining ruins of a stone house. A plaque has been erected and tells the story of a government official called Lanthrop Brown and his wife. They acquired the land in 1924 and built the stone house. At that time, they became friends with Julia Pfeiffer Burns and remained so until her death in 1928. In their 1961 bequest to the State of California, they dedicated the property to her memory and so explaining how the park came to be known as the Julia Pfeiffer Burns State Park.

We make our way back along the trail, drinking in more views of McWay falls along the way.

It's now scorching hot, obviously welcomed by Shelby whose trousers have now completely dried.

Plaskett Creek and Sand Dollar Beach

We make our way further down Big Sur to Plaskett Creek, which is to be the site for our third night.

We turn into a wooded area surrounded by large Monterey pine trees. There's a mixture of tents and trailers parked up among the trees, but it isn't at all as crowded as the KOA campsite.

We stop to book in with the lady who runs the campsite and to buy some firewood.

Despite it being pretty hot during the day time, the temperature drops in the evening. Having a stock of firewood is a must, and everyone else obviously thinks the same thing.

'Firewood is totally out,' Tom says as he gets back into the van. 'Lady says that she should have another load delivered in about an hour, and I can go back then and pick some up.'

We drive along the trail through the pine trees until we find our camp spot.

'We are near the bathrooms,' Shelby announces, pointing in the direction of a single-storey building about fifteen yards from our camp.

'Not sure if that's a good thing or a bad thing,' I say. I feel like I could write a guide to camping bathrooms, having come across such a variation of extremes along the way already.

We now decide that Tom, the tour guide, is to be renamed 'pack man' because he has been packing and de-packing the van down to a fine art.

He climbs the ladder and begins to unpack the roof rack.

We realise there needs to be some order in preparing the tent for when it was dark, and so we all have our own system of ensuring our bags have the things we need for the night and the morning at the top.

We have also appointed a wash bag, which is growing by the day, mainly due to Leon, who somehow manages to soak or ruin at least one set of clothing every day.

We now have so much sand on board that we can easily recreate a beach right in front of the tent!

Fortunately for us, however, Sand Dollar Beach is literally just across the road. We agree that once we have the beach gear off the van, I'll take the kids to the beach. Shelby and Tom are going to set up the tent and join us later.

'You do not want to go in there often,' Vanessa shouts, appearing from the toilet block.

'No showers, just the grossest toilets you have *ever* seen in your life,' she says, distorting the features of her face, obviously totally disgusted with her recent experience.

'I haven't been for a number two since we left home,' Shelby announces, 'and it's highly possible that tonight is the night,' she says, looking worried.

'Well, honey, thanks for sharing that with us,' Tom says and laughs.

'I'm serious, Tom. I haven't been for three days, and it's not funny!' she says, sounding quite concerned.

'I actually really need to go, all that water we drank on the way. I'll go investigate. I mean how bad can it be?' I say, heading up to the toilet.

The campsite is totally covered by an umbrella of trees, making everywhere a lot darker than it actually is.

There are no lights in the toilets, and as I walk through the door, I realise that Vanessa was actually putting it mildly with her statement about not wanting to go in there often; how about never!

As I enter, I notice that the floor is wet, but kind of slimy wet. To the left is a single toilet with a metal door and to the right, the same but with a slightly lower door.

I decide to take a deep breath and look. After all, I can hardly go squat behind a tree, can I? There are far too many people about, and besides, I am too worried about what might pop up out of the grass and bite my bum.

I take a step to the left and push open the toilet door. It's pretty dark and nothing much to see but a wet-looking floor and a dark-looking smelly toilet.

Despite this, and the smell being enough to put you off ever going to the toilet again, a woman is standing in front of the single sink unit, in between the two toilets, brushing her teeth. Yes, brushing her teeth! How anyone can brush their teeth in the middle of two of the smelliest toilets ever is just beyond me.

The smell is overpowering. I walk to the right and look in the second toilet. It's pretty much the same, although the toilet itself looks cleaner. I wonder whether there is just more light this side of the building. I really need to stop my toilet survey and just go!

I decide the 'lighter toilet' is the lesser of the two evils.

I do my usual half standing half sitting hover above the toilet seat and hope I can pee fast. I glance on the floor to see something move. A worm! Totally gross or what! A worm, slithering around on the slimy floor! And probably nothing like the usual earth worms that live in soil either.

I hurry and run out of the toilet block, looking like a woman possessed, squealing with my arms flailing around me.

'Where's the hand stuff?' I say, running to the van and frantically rummaging through my bag.

Tom laughs. 'Toilet's that great then, Grace?'

'You do not want to go in there at all, never mind often. There is a worm on the floor, a worm!' I cry, hardly believing it myself.

'Grace, we are camping,' Tom says, rather matter of factly. 'The toilets aren't unclean. They are just more outdoor kind of toilets and used by a lot of people camping, so there's bound to be more dirt. You'll get used to it,' he says, jumping down from the van.

'I doubt that very much,' I say, madly rubbing the antibacterial gel into my hands.

'The only upside to those kind of toilets is the fact your thigh muscles become stronger from the squatting position I have to get myself in so I don't have to sit down fully on the seat to pee!'

Tom laughs.

'I'm with you on that one, and I am dreading going in there,' Shelby says.

'Right guys, come on,' I shout over to Sam, Vanessa, and Leon. 'Let's go find the beach.'

We grab some towels and the beach mats and make our way out of the camp.

After crossing the road, we find a path that leads to the top of the beach. It's a long way down, probably over 100 feet. The path winds its way down and then stops at some steps that drop very steeply down on to the beach.

The view is amazing, and we are excited to get down on to the beach.

The tide is quite a long way out, and the beach pretty deserted, so we pick a good spot, and Vanessa and Leon run out to the sea.

'I'm going to just sit here awhile,' Sam says.

With such high cliffs behind us, the beach is a suntrap, and it feels hot. I obviously welcome the hot afternoon sun but poor Sam clearly doesn't.

'You'll feel cooler if you are by the surf,' I say, trying to encourage him to join Vanessa and Leon.

'Okay,' he says, 'maybe you're right.' And he jumps up to join them.

I lay back on the beach mat, enjoying the sun warming my face.

The screams pierce the silence.

I look over to where the kids are and see Sam hopping up and down, crying.

I jump up and run over to them.

'What's happened?' I say, unable to figure out what's going on.

Sam is distressed and obviously in pain.

'I got stung by a bee,' he says, crying.

'It's okay,' I say, trying to calm him down. 'It'll be fine. Let's go back and sit down so I can take a look.'

He sits down on the towel, and I look at his foot. I can't see anything.

'Are you sure?' I say.

'Yes, I saw it lying on the sand afterwards. There were a bunch of them around us.'

'He did get stung, Mum, but it looked like a wasp to me,' Vanessa says.

'No, it was a bee!' Sam says indignantly.

The bees in America generally look like our wasps. They call the bees we have in England bumblebees, or at least, that's what I've figured out.

So I guess that to Vanessa it was a wasp and to Sam it was definitely a bee. Either way, it has obviously stung him. Having never been stung before, I can't relate to his pain, but I remember my elder brother being trapped in a telephone box with a bee. Suffice to say, he never made the call, and the bee never made it out.

Sam lies down on his towel and says he is going to sleep for a while. I feel so bad for him and am sure he'll feel better when Shelby arrives. Mums always make everything better, don't they?

Vanessa and Leon go back to the sea and begin writing their names in the wet sand.

Tom and Shelby appear soon after, and we relay the bee-stinging story. Sam is not a happy bunny.

'I might do some yoga,' I say, eager to have a practice.

With the cold mornings and evenings, I haven't really had chance to practise, and we've been driving and visiting places during the day so it seems a good time, with it feeling so hot.

'I don't have a mat, but I could use one of the beach mats,' I say, rolling it up.

'We'll watch Vanessa and Leon. Why don't you go over there?' Shelby says, pointing further down the beach. 'Then maybe some surfer dude will spot you and come over to chat.'

More people have now arrived on the beach and because the surf is so good, there are quite a lot of surfers.

'Yeah, right,' I say, feeling a bit old for some of the surfers who all look to be twenty teen!

'I'll be focusing on yoga, not the surfers,' I say, smiling at Shelby and then stick my tongue out at Tom, who is laughing.

I pull my shorts over my bikini bottoms. I don't mind so much about the top half of me because I have no chest to actually fall out of my bikini top. I don't feel too comfortable without shorts over my bikini bottoms however, and knowing me, I'll end up accidentally catching the string and undoing the whole lot. Oh, what a sight that would be!

I walk further along the beach and find a flat spot of sand in front of some rocks and lay out the beach mat.

I start practising sun salutations, and as I lie down on the mat, realise I am not alone.

There are literally hundreds of tiny bugs jumping around like fleas beneath me.

Gorgeous sandy white beach, Pacific Ocean, azure blue sky, beautiful sunshine, and bugs! They just don't fit into that equation, do they?

What are they? I continue with the sun salutations, trying to ignore them. They aren't really big enough that I can feel them; they're tiny, but big enough to see. I look closer; they're almost transparent and more than that, I wonder if they are going to do me any harm!

A few yards away from me, some seaweed has washed on to the shore, and I can see that it's literally covered in the same tiny bugs. They're everywhere!

I choose to ignore them and carry on with my practice, trying to remember the sagely yogic advice of breathing in and out through the nose, keeping my mouth firmly shut, just in case!

I am thrilled at having done some yoga on the beach, even though Shelby says she would have been more thrilled had the surfers, who wandered by staring at me, stopped to speak.

I feel too old to be flirting with surfers. I am almost thirty-seven, for goodness sake! Had this been twenty years ago, it might have been a different story, and I am sure I am at least that much older than them, anyway!

We make our way back to the campsite, and I offer to go and collect the firewood.

I can't say I can recall the last time I was put in charge of a wheelbarrow, but the lady in charge of the site suggests I take the barrow at the front and help myself to the wood we've bought.

It's seriously hard work, trying to steer a wheelbarrow heavy with firewood. It's a bit like when you were little and experienced speed wobbles on your bike from going downhill too fast, except on this occasion, I am going downhill in charge of a barrow full of wood!

The barrow is going far too fast for me, and I struggle to keep up.

Shelby, who offered to walk with me, is laughing hysterically as she watches me run faster, my knees bent in an attempt to keep some control over the wayward wheelbarrow.

I crash through the campsite much to Tom's amusement and land by the fire.

We empty the wood but then reload it just so Shelby can take a photograph of me with the barrow loaded up with wood.

'Just look at my trainers!' I say, sitting down on one of the camp chairs after taking the wheelbarrow back. 'They're grey!' I exclaim, looking down at my feet.

Vanessa, Leon, and I all have sparkling white trainers. Well, they were when we arrived. They are now tinged a shade of grey from all the dirt and dust in the campgrounds. Much to Tom's amusement, of course.

'That's just camping, Grace. Put your flip-flops on, instead,' he suggests.

'Yeah, right, and have my feet this dirty, I don't think so.'

'Mine are grey too,' Leon says rather proudly.

'And mine,' Vanessa adds.

'Yes, yes, okay,' I say, waving my arms.

'I need to become at one with the dirt,' I say, holding my hands out, with my finger touching my thumb: the mudra (hand gesture) symbolising oneness.

Tom and Shelby burst out laughing.

'You'll get used to it, and maybe next time you might try old trainers or walking boots,' Tom says.

'I like white trainers, or I did, before they went grey, anyway.'

Later, after going out for dinner, we arrive back at camp and light the fire, settling down to enjoy our nightly dose of S'mores. I don't think I will ever get bored with them and am now averaging two or three a night!

Tom heads down to the tent with the lantern to sort the sleeping bags out before Leon goes to bed.

'Tom!' Shelby booms at the top of her voice. 'Lantern *now!*'

'What's wrong?' Tom says worriedly, running back from the tent, handing Shelby the lantern.

Without a word, Shelby grabs the lantern and races up towards the toilet building.

'Oh, dear,' Tom says, 'guess three days is long enough.'

'Yes, and she'll wish she went four after needing to go in there,' I say, not wanting to go in there myself now it's dark.

We have all managed to avoid going to the toilet until it's absolutely necessary.

After several minutes, Shelby reappears.

'Oh, that was awful,' she groans, looking rather pale. 'I don't go for days and of all the places I have the real need to go, it's here.'

'I'll get the hand gel,' I say, and we all laugh.

Tom and I usually get up around 5.00 a.m.

Not sure what it is with our family, but we all tend to be very early risers.

We decide to make the most of the early morning and walk across the road down to the beach.

I've never walked on a beach this early in the morning, and it's as though someone has just picked up a paintbrush and painted the scene. Everything is touched with a hue of violet blue: the sand, the sky, and the sea. It's so serene and peaceful.

We walk as far as we can see in one direction before the cliffs prevent us from going any further, and then do the same in the other direction.

We come to a spot where when the sea comes in, you can't pass beyond it, but when it goes back, you can make your way across.

Of course, I follow Tom without realising what I am doing, and then turn back to see that where we have just come from is impassable because the sea has come back in. This makes me slightly nervous, I have to admit.

We are now clambering over rocks which are becoming a little tricky and so decide to turn back.

'Just come across when the sea is out,' Tom calls as he walks back.

'Right,' I say nervously, trying to clamber back across the rocks.

I climb a little too high and then realise I can't make it back across because the sea is coming in. I decide to climb a little higher and make my way over the rocks rather than across the sand, with the sea to contend with.

'Tom!' I yell now, unable to see him.

The rocks are really sharp, and rather than continuing to yell, I figure I should concentrate on getting across them.

'Grace!' I hear Tom shout.

I slip a few times and catch my heart in my throat, clear a few more rocks, and see Tom on the sand below me.

'What are you doing up there?' he says.

'Oh, you know, I just thought I would rather climb over jagged rocks. What do you think? I went up too high and couldn't get back across before the sea came back in. I was worried there for a minute,' I say, jumping down the last few rocks to where Tom was standing.

'Let's get back, shall we, before we lose you altogether?' Tom says, running ahead.

Vanessa, Leon, and Sam greet us when we arrive back into camp.

Although Vanessa shows a vague interest in yoga, she isn't anywhere near as much into it as Leon.

Since watching David Swenson, one of the world's foremost teachers of Ashtanga yoga, on a DVD I have at home, he's been hooked. He often takes out *The Practice Manual*, performing each of the postures in turn.

I am convinced he'll grow into a great yogi some day, and he's now making the most of his talent by showing Sam how to perform the Tree and Warrior II while standing on a log.

Not one to be left out, Vanessa joins in, and what a great picture it makes with the three of them performing the Tree while balancing on one!

We stop at another beautiful restaurant along the coast and enjoy yet another delicious breakfast of waffles, pancakes, and fresh fruit.

Despite being on a camping trip, I have never eaten so well. I haven't eaten a bad meal since I arrived, and it seems to be getting better by the day. I wish I could say the same for the toilets!

Mum's birthday is shortly after we get back from the camping trip, so we make the most of the gift shop and buy her a couple of birthday presents.

Our next stop is Hearst Castle, which is located just outside the city of San Simeon.

We pull into the car park and, much to Tom's delight, park right next to a tan VW Vanagon.

It's blisteringly hot, and after smothering sun cream on ourselves and the kids, we head up to the visitor centre.

Shelby pre-booked our tour. We don't have to wait long before we are shown to our bus, which is to take us five miles inland to reach the castle.

Hearst Castle is located at 1,600 feet, on top of a hill in the Santa Lucia Mountains. It was built on a 250,000-acre ranch that William Randolph Hearst, a media mogul, commissioned architect Julia Morgan to design in 1919.

What began as a comfortable single-storey house turned into an enormous estate, comprising 90,080 square feet to include Casa Grande, the main house and three guest houses Casa Del Sol, Casa Del Mar, and Casa Del Monte, totalling fifty-six bedrooms, sixty-one bathrooms, and nineteen sitting rooms.

The estate also features indoor and outdoor pools, a movie theatre, tennis courts, an airfield, 127 acres of gardens, and the world's largest private zoo!

When you say you are going to take a castle tour in England, you expect to be pretty chilly as you wander around crumbling stone buildings, usually followed by a trip down into the dungeons.

When the tour bus arrives, we can't believe what we are seeing. It's as though someone just planted us in the middle of the best estate in Hollywood. White marble statues are everywhere, beautiful gardens, with exotic flowers, waterfalls, exquisite art, and the finest architecture I have ever seen in my life. Everything screams opulence, luxury, lavishness, and style.

The castle looks out to the Pacific Ocean, and the land around the castle is unspoiled, making the views spectacular.

William Hearst liked to entertain; his frequent Hollywood guests included Charlie Chaplin, Cary Grant, Greta Garbo, Bob Hope, and Clark

Gable, and the most important political figures of the time, including the New York City Mayor Jimmy Walker and Winston Churchill.

The highlights of the tour for me are the outdoor and indoor pools.

The Neptune Pool took twelve years to complete, having been rebuilt three times, finally measuring 104 feet long and 58 feet wide (95 feet wide if you were to measure into the alcove!), holding just under 350,000 gallons of water. The centrepiece is the front of a roman building that William Hearst imported to California. It is the most beautiful swimming pool I have ever seen, and the only downside is that it is scorching hot, and we are only permitted to look at the pool, not experience it.

The tour guide informs us that someone has fallen into the pool in the past. I wonder if they had not been able to resist the temptation and just jumped in rather than fell. That I could relate to.

I ask the guide whether anyone ever uses the pool any more. He says that once a year, a number of employees win the chance to use it for a day.

The jury is still out on my opinion about preservation vs experience. It seems such a huge shame that all that beauty is there just to be adored, rather than really experienced and enjoyed. I can, however, see that without preservation, the castle, including the pools, won't last very long. Nothing is meant to last forever though, is it?

The indoor pool, the Roman Pool, was modelled on a roman bath and is nothing short of utterly spectacular. The entire room appears blue and gold, including the pool itself, and is covered in tiny one-inch, blue-and-orange tiles. The glistening gold, our tour guide tells us, is achieved by fusing gold inside clear tiles. We are walking with gold beneath our feet! Eight marble statues of Greek gods and goddesses adorn the pool.

Sadly, this sees the end of our tour, but we are buzzing from the experience and thrilled that Shelby and Tom thought to include it on our trip.

Morro Rock and Gaviota Beach

Apart from Tom showering with a frog, our stay at a San Simeon campsite is pretty uneventful.

Back on the road again, we make our way to Morro Rock, a 581-foot volcanic plug, which is basically a volcanic landform created when the magma hardened.

We make a quick stop off so I can transfer my daily growing number of photographs from my camera to disk and pull into the parking lot by Morro Rock shortly after.

Morro Rock forms part of the Nine Sisters, which are a chain of twelve volcanic peaks between Morro Bay and San Luis Obispo.

The twelve peaks, including the one we are now standing next to, were formed 12,000,000 (yes, you did read that right, 12 million!) years ago.

With the beach right in front of us, Vanessa, Sam, and Leon decide to play in the sand. We all need the bathroom, but I say I can go before we leave and will stay and watch the kids while Tom and Shelby go.

There are two guys unloading their surfboards off the back of their truck at the side of the van.

With Shelby's words ringing in my ears about 'just practising', I decide to seize the opportunity and practise a little harmless flirtation.

One of them looks over and smiles. I feel a bit of an idiot, standing here, smiling like a dribbling lunatic, but what the heck and smile back.

Feeling rather confident, I am about to say 'hi' when something white catches my eye. Hanging out the side of the front pocket on my bright blue fleece is a bright white Tampax® for all the world to see!

Oh, the embarrassment! Now I do feel like an idiot.

I duck around the van, jump in the front seat, pull the tampoon (tampoon is a synonym we have for a tampon and came about when I tried to explain what they were to Vanessa) out of my pocket, and stuff it into my bag.

Tom and Shelby return from the bathroom, and we walk over to get a closer look at Morro Rock.

I relay my embarrassing incident to Shelby, who can't stop laughing.

'It's just so funny,' she says between fits of laughter. 'You finally pluck up the courage to go flirt with someone, and you have a tampoon hanging out of your pocket.' She is almost crying with laughter.

'Come on then,' Tom says. 'Share the joke.'

'Well, it's a bit embarrassing to tell your brother this, but it can't be any more embarrassing than what happened.'

I tell Tom about the tampoon, and he roars with laughter.

'Only you, Grace, only you,' he says, still laughing.

I have to laugh; I can't help it. I mean, how ridiculous must I have looked giving it the big 'look at me' and acting all cool with a great tampoon hanging out of my pocket. It wasn't like you couldn't see it either, because it was super, so bigger than the normal ones and in a white packet that was a stark contrast against my bright blue fleece!

We take photos of each other standing in front of the rock, and then Shelby takes one, standing almost back at the van to give some size proportions.

Still laughing about the tampoon incident, we drive out of the car park.

'I'm scared for life,' I say to Tom and Shelby. 'I'll never flirt again!'

They both laugh.

'Morro Rock is no more,' Tom says. 'It has a new name now . . . "Tampoon Point"!'

We stop off for an early lunch at the Rock and Roll Diner, which is a restaurant housed in a long silver train car (well, two attached together, I think). Definitely rock and roll and very fifties diner style with a jukebox, neon signs, red-and-white checked vinyl, and lots of fifties memorabilia and music playing.

Now singing along to Elvis, we order our drinks.

Shelby points out that the waiter is obviously quite taken with me.

'Oh no!' I say. 'Hasn't my last tale of flirting woe done enough damage to my reputation for one day?' I ask pleadingly.

'Of course not!' she says, laughing.

'Not a prayer,' I say. 'And besides, he is most definitely not my type.'

'What is your type then?' Tom asks, looking rather serious. 'Surfers?'

He and Shelby fall about laughing.

I try to hide my smile. 'Yes, that's it,' I say, trying to sound serious. 'Have your jokes on me.'

Having evaded more flirting disasters, we finish lunch and hit the road again.

As tomorrow is my birthday, Tom says that the next destination will be a surprise.

'All I will tell you, Grace, is that it's just what you asked for,' he says. I'm intrigued but like surprises, so don't ask further.

We turn off the highway and arrive at a check point. 'Gaviota State Park,' the sign reads.

'This is it,' Tom says. 'A campsite right by the beach.'

'Ah, thanks, this is fantastic!' I squeal, hardly able to contain my excitement.

Many months ago, I'd spoken to Tom on the phone, and he had said that he wanted to plan this camping trip, and he was saying that he wanted to make sure it gave everyone something. I said that I didn't mind what we did, but that it would be great if I could wake up by the beach on my birthday.

The trip has obviously overdelivered on being by the ocean because every day we have either been on it or driving alongside it. Most nights we have been close enough to the ocean to be able to hear the waves crashing onto the shore, but this is just amazing; we are camping right by Gaviota Beach!

Unpacking the van and putting up the tent now takes less than an hour. We are all getting used to living out of one bag too, and Tom has even consolidated our bags down to just two. We're doing well!

We become a little concerned by the guy camping right beside us, who appears to be drinking from a whisky bottle and happily talking to himself.

'The guy from the KOA campsite followed us,' Tom whispers.

'It wouldn't surprise me,' I say, looking over at the man worrying whether he will be bothering us during the night.

'He seems harmless enough, just enjoying camping and drinking, I think,' Shelby says.

We set up camp for the fifth time and walk towards the beach, stopping off at the little shop in the campsite along the way.

'Can I have a board, Mum, pleeeease?' Leon pleads.

The shop sells body boards, which are the perfect size for Leon. He is so in awe of the surfers we have seen riding the waves over the past few days; he just wants to have a go himself.

Vanessa and Sam try to tell him that he can't stand up on a body board, but he isn't having any of it.

'If I want to stand up on it, I can,' he says, as I'm paying for it.

'Of course, you can do whatever you want on it so long as you have your life vest on though, okay?' I say.

'See!' he says, turning around to pull a face at Vanessa.

The beach is great, but Leon is a little cautious about getting into the water on his board.

'Would it help if I showed you?' Tom says, offering to be the first one to go in.

'Yes!' Leon cries. 'And then I'll have a go,' he says excitedly.

Tom makes his way into the water to show Leon how it's done.

After ten minutes, Leon says that he wants to try but can't quite get to grips with putting his body on the board, quite happy to just stand on the board and catch the tide coming in to the shore.

Tom and Shelby say they are going back to the van so Tom can change.

I settle back to catch the last rays of the afternoon sun while Vanessa, Sam, and Leon play in the surf. Each time they run in and out of the surf, they move a little further up the beach.

'Guys!' I yell. 'Don't go too far.'

'Okay, Mum,' Vanessa shouts back, waving.

I hear screaming and instinctively know it's one of them. What is it with us and beaches!

'Mum!' Vanessa cries between sobs. I look over to see them all running towards me, soaked from head to toe.

'The sea took us under,' Leon blurts out, jumping down on to a towel.

'Yeah, this big wave came and took us under, and it nearly swept us out to sea,' Sam continues.

'I hurt my ankle on a rock,' Vanessa says, crying. 'I thought I was going to drown.'

She sits down next to me to show me her ankle.

'Well, it looks fine, but you need to be careful out there. Maybe you should stay right in front of this spot, rather than walking up the beach too far,' I suggest.

'But I could have drowned, Mum!' Vanessa says seriously, holding her ankle.

'I know, sweetie, but you didn't. Thank goodness!' I say, giving her a hug.

Tom and Shelby return and Sam gives them the whole story on how the now monster wave came over them and nearly took them under.

We make the most of the sun and then decide to go and find somewhere to eat.

We find a restaurant, which is famous for its pea and ham soup.

Being vegetarian, I don't get to sample the delicacy but doubt I would have tried it, anyway.

Once upon a time when I was younger, my mum went through this stage, obviously at my dad's request, of cooking home-made pea soup. The smell that permeated the house was overwhelming, and the thought of eating something runny and green was just revolting. I am suddenly reminded of that smell and decide there will be no peas for me tonight.

There's a large store as we enter the restaurant, and Vanessa, not surprisingly, manages to find something she falls in love with. A 'real' puppy, complete with soft carry case and broken leg.

'Pleeeeeease, can I have it?' Vanessa says, tugging my arm.

'We're here for dinner, not toys,' I say, trying to steer her in the opposite direction.

'But just look at it,' she pleads.

'Okay,' I say, sighing and letting her lead me to where the puppy is.

It does look real. It's even breathing! It has some mechanism in its tummy that makes it go up and down, like a real dog would when it's sleeping. It's about nine inches long and lying down on a blanket. Its injured back paw has a pink bandage wrapped around it, which yells 'feel sorry for me and buy me'. It works a treat on convincing Vanessa.

Although I've already bought her birthday gifts, it's also worked a treat on me too, and I decide I'll somehow buy it, without her knowing.

'Let's leave it for now,' I say, trying to ease her pleading.

'Okay, but can we come back after dinner and get it then?' she says.

'I don't know, Vanessa. Let's just have dinner, shall we?' I say, ushering her through to the restaurant.

We sit down to order, and I whisper to Shelby that I want to get Vanessa the puppy. Tom hands me the keys under the table, and I say I am going to the bathroom.

I buy the puppy, stash it in the back of the van, and hurry back to the table.

'You were a long time, Mummy,' Vanessa says. She's such a detective!

'There was a queue for the bathroom, sweetie,' I say, rather nonchalantly.

We finish dinner and decide to take a look around the store.

'It's gone!' Vanessa yells, bursting into tears.

She's inconsolable, and I feel awful, knowing that I've bought the puppy but can't tell her that and ruin the surprise for her birthday.

'I guess they sold it,' Tom says, giving her a hug. 'We'll find another one. I've seen them in other stores,' he says, trying to make her feel better.

'I'm not surprised someone bought it. It was lovely, and I wanted it so much,' she says, whimpering.

She spends the whole time we are browsing the shop with a sad face, and each time any of us try to speak to her, she starts crying again.

On the drive to our next destination, Tom continues to convince her that he has seen it in other stores and is sure as soon as we return home, he'll find one for her.

Although she is still reliving the awful moment when she went back to see the puppy after dinner and it was gone, Tom's promise of finding her the puppy when we return home is enough to appease her for the time being.

When we arrive back to camp, Tom starts a fire, and Shelby begins preparing the chocolate and biscuits for S'mores. We are now all hopelessly addicted to them and justify our huge consumption with the fact that we are on a camping trip and probably won't have them again for some considerable time to come.

We sit around the campfire, toasting our marshmallows.

'What's that?' Vanessa says, sounding spooked.

'What?' Tom responds.

Sam, who loves spooky stories, makes the most of the opportunity.

'Maybe it's a ghost,' he says.

Vanessa wails. 'I don't like ghosts,' she says.

'It's not a ghost,' Tom says, rolling his eyes at Sam.

We all listen and hear a rustle in the bushes.

I am closest to the bushes and leap off my chair.

'There's something moving in there! I just saw something!' I shriek, moving away from the fire.

'It's a raccoon,' Tom says, peering further into the bushes. 'Maybe he wants some S'mores,' he says, laughing. 'There he goes, look,' Tom says, pointing away from the bushes. 'I think your leaping out of the chair scared him half to death.'

'Scared me half to death more like,' Vanessa says.

'You and me both,' I say and look over to where Tom was pointing but can't see anything.

'Let's sit back down and finish these S'mores, unless you don't want to now,' Tom says.

'Yeah, right,' Shelby says, and we all laugh.

Fifteenth of July

'Happy birthday, Grace,' Tom says as I pop my head out of the tent.

He's already up and making coffee.

'Thanks!' I reply cheerfully, excited that it's my birthday.

I've always loved my birthday, and even though I am now thirty-seven, I still get just as excited as I did when I was seven. Whenever I've been at work, I have always booked the day off and done something nice for the day, and the sun has always shone. Well, of course, it would; it's St Swithin's Day. According to form (my mum always quotes form, but I have no idea who form is or where it comes from, just that form is usually right), if it rains on St Swithin's Day, it rains for forty days. For thirty-seven years, I actually thought that form in this case was the Bible, Genesis to be precise, referring to where Noah built his ark and rain fell on the earth for forty days and forty nights.

Later in my thirty-sixth year, however, I discovered that St Swithin was actually the bishop of Winchester! At his request, he was buried outside his church, where his body would be subject to the raindrops from up high. Some years later, it was decided to move his body to an indoor shrine, and on the day of the move, tremendous rain ensued. It was believed this was the bishop showing his displeasure at being moved, and from there, the weather lore began.

You learn something new every day!

'I'm going to have a shower but won't be long,' I say, getting my things together and heading off to the shower block.

The showers are spacious, clean, and with no mass murderers, frogs or worms in sight, I feel quite happy to be having a lovely hot shower on the morning of my birthday.

'Happy Birthday!' Vanessa and Leon sing in unison as I arrive back to camp.

'Sit down, Mummy,' Vanessa instructs. Tom hands me some coffee, and Shelby comes out of the van.

'Morning! Happy Birthday, Grace,' she says, giving me a hug.

With everyone now sitting around the fire Tom has made, Vanessa begins handing out gifts.

What a perfect way to start a birthday: by the ocean in front of a warm campfire.

Everyone bursts into song.

'Happy birthday to you! Happy birthday to you, happy birthday dear Mummy/Grace, happy birthday to you!'

'Thank you!' I cry excitedly, clapping my hands and reaching for the presents.

Leon gives me a beautiful Buddha pen and Vanessa a photograph of the Golden Gate Bridge.

I laugh when I open one of the gifts from Shelby and Tom: a mug that has 'I'm single' in bright blue letters around it and then 'not desperate' written underneath.

'Only you!' I say to Shelby.

'Well, I thought you need to get drinking out of that mug because any cute guy passing by will then know you are single without you having to put out the vibe,' she says.

'Right, so I'll just walk along with mug in hand then, shall I?' I say, laughing.

'No, silly! But, you know, when we are hanging about, get the mug out. Hey, that rhymes!' Shelby exclaims.

I burst out laughing, and Tom shakes his head.

'Should never have told her you wanted to meet someone,' he says.

'I'm just helping her along,' Shelby says defensively.

'I know you are,' Tom says hugging her. 'I'm only teasing you.'

Shelby bought me a dress, which she gives me as a present from Sam, which I saw in one of the stores on the Santa Cruz boardwalk.

'I love this dress!' I say, surprised, reaching over to hug Sam. 'I didn't even realise you had gone back to get it.'

'We were sneaky and trailed behind you when we were walking back to the van. We just ran in and bought it,' Shelby says, 'I'm really glad you like it.'

The dress is just me, with a peace sign on the front.

After finishing opening my birthday presents and cards, we start packing up.

'We're off to Disneyland!' Tom says excitedly.

'Yay!' Vanessa, Sam, and Leon yell together.

Shelby and Tom booked us all into the original Disneyland Hotel for two nights. We are going to arrive there midafternoon and then go out to dinner to celebrate my birthday, and then tomorrow on Vanessa's tenth birthday, we'll spend the day in the Disneyland Park, followed by another dinner and overnight stay.

Shelby has taken care of booking the whole thing and after camping all week, we are all, well, with the exception of Tom, who is a hard core camper, excited at the prospect of beds, pillows, luxury, and comfort.

'I might sleep in the van,' Tom says.

'You will not!' Shelby says. 'I've been looking forward to this all week.'

'Mainstream hotel, thousands of people, blistering heat, can't wait,' Tom says with a hint of sarcasm.

'You'll live,' Shelby says, nudging him.

Vanessa and Leon befriend a Corgi by the name of Sally who belongs to the people who are camping alongside us. Sally laps up the fuss and Vanessa is delighted to spend some quality time with a dog.

We say our goodbyes to Gaviota Beach and hit the highway, heading inland towards Los Angeles.

Disneyland and Vanessa's Tenth Birthday

The closer we get to Los Angeles, the heavier the traffic becomes.

Of all the past few days, this is probably the longest time we have spent travelling in the van.

We finally arrive midafternoon and stop to take a photograph of the palm-tree flanked entrance wall, welcoming us to the Disneyland Hotel.

We make our way to the entrance where Tom unloads the bags and drops us off. A man appears immediately, offering to park the van but Tom declines.

'As if I am going to let someone park my van,' he says.

Shelby rolls her eyes.

One of the porters comes with a trolley and loads the bags while Tom parks the van.

As we enter the lobby, there's a wall-length mural of Sleeping Beauty's castle and bronze statues of Mickey and Minnie Mouse mounted on marble blocks either side.

While Shelby and Tom go off to check in, Vanessa, Sam, Leon, and I take some photographs.

The hotel is a Three Diamond Deluxe hotel and is magical, lavish, and luxurious. It probably seems even more so to us having spent a week camping!

We take the elevator to the eleventh floor and set about finding our rooms. Shelby has booked two adjoining rooms, which both have two queen-sized beds. Antonio and Kate are driving down to Los Angeles to spend tomorrow with us.

'Wow!' Vanessa and Leon exclaim as we enter the room.

They have never really stayed in a big hotel before, and so this is a really exciting experience for them.

'Look at the beds,' Vanessa says. 'And the TV!' she cries.

Sleeping Beauty's castle is painted on the headboards and doors of the TV cabinet.

Shelby comes through the adjoining door.

'Like your room, guys?' she says.

'We have chocolates!' Leon exclaims, picking up the complimentary chocolates which are on the turned down sheets. 'Can we eat them?' he says, already unwrapping one.

"Course but share with Vanessa and Sam,' I say.

We celebrate my birthday at the Rainforest Cafe® in Downtown Disney®. It's a great adventure for the kids because as the name suggests, the whole restaurant is decked out as a rainforest. Every fifteen minutes or so thunder cracks and the lights go low and lots of different model animals that are scattered around the restaurant start to move.

We head back to the hotel and end the night, watching fireworks from the balcony window.

'They must have known it was my birthday,' I say as we watch the fireworks fill the sky.

'Don't know about them, but we did,' Shelby says, appearing with a birthday cake.

Everyone sings again, and I pretend to blow out the candles. Shelby has been instructed by concierge that it's against fire regulations to have lit candles in guest rooms, and there's a severe fine for setting off the smoke alarm. We aren't going to chance it.

Vanessa and Leon are fast asleep the second their heads hit the pillows, and I'm not too far behind them. The pillows are like marshmallow, and it's hard to believe we are actually sleeping in beds: huge queen-size beds!

Vanessa is still sleeping when I wake up. I shower and gather together her presents which Tom bought in and hid the night before. Leon wakes up, and we decide to wake Vanessa.

'Happy birthday, Vanessa,' Leon says, whispering in her ear.

She sleepily opens her eyes.

'Happy birthday!' we all cry.

'We're going to Disneyland today!' Leon says excitedly.

Vanessa sits up, and Leon hands her some gifts while I grab the camera.

She reaches for the gift bag containing the puppy she has seen at the restaurant. As she moves the tissue paper and sees a glance of the carry case, she knows and promptly bursts into tears.

'The puppy!' she cries. 'I've never cried in happiness before,' she says, taking the case out of the bag.

'I love it so much. I'm going to name him Marlo,' she says, pulling out the adoption certificate that came with the puppy.

'Open the rest of your gifts. Then we'll get you a pen, and you can fill it in,' I say, handing her some more gifts.

Leon and I bought her a digital camera, and she is excited to start taking photographs right away.

'I'll go put it on charge. Now let's get ready for Disneyland, shall we?' I say.

We are planning on leaving at 7.30 a.m. because the park opens at 8.00 a.m., and if we go early, we won't have to queue for too long.

We manage to leave on time and walk through Downtown Disney to get to the park.

Vanessa is given a special birthday badge, and with all our passes, we head towards Main Street.

'Welcome to the magic,' Tom says.

We walk towards Sleeping Beauty's Castle and decide we'll take the kids on some rides before meeting up with Antonio and Kate.

We walk through the castle gates, and two women dressed as Sleeping Beauty and Cinderella give us a leaflet for the Bibbidi Bobbidi Boutique, which is basically a makeover salon for little girls. They go in as themselves and come out as princesses, complete with hair, make-up, and outfits.

Vanessa says she would love to go, and so while we are queuing for one of the rides, I phone and book her a lunchtime appointment. As a birthday treat, she's going to have her hair and make-up done.

Leon's favourite ride is the Pirates of the Caribbean, which we only manage to pull him away from, with the promise of returning later with Antonio and Kate.

Kate calls, and so we make our way back to Main Street to meet up with them.

'Hey!' shouts Antonio, 'fancy seeing you here.'

'Happy birthday,' Kate says, hugging Vanessa. 'I have your gift back at the hotel so you can open that later.'

We all hug and decide to visit the Haunted Mansion® before finding some roller coasters to ride before lunch. I'm not entirely sure whether I want to ride roller coasters at all but decide to give them the once-over before taking the plunge and joining the queue.

At the age of eight, I remember eagerly jumping on a huge Ferris wheel at a local fair and then screaming my head off to get let off when it stopped and we were sitting swinging at the top. The man had to quickly stop the ride to let me get off.

I've managed to avoid any kind of fair rides until I was a teenager, when I was talked into getting on the waltzer, which basically spins around so fast it makes your head spin and your stomach wants to throw up. Why is that considered fun, is all I can ask. After that I decided that fast rides weren't for me, but once again, some years later, was talked into going to a theme park and did venture on a few roller coasters and miraculously managed to survive.

I have realised my fear isn't so much speed, it's heights.

'I'll go on one if it's not too high,' I say, trying to convince myself more than anyone else.

'Well, if Vanessa and Leon can go on them, then I am sure you can,' Tom says.

'I'm not going,' Sam says. 'They make me feel sick.'

'I know how you feel,' I say to Sam.

'We're in Disneyland, and that means rides!' Tom says excitedly. 'Now let's go find some,' he says, bounding off in front.

We go on as many as we can.

The Haunted Mansion terrifies Vanessa right from the start. As we enter the mansion, we are ushered into an octagonal room which then begins moving as though the room is stretching. It's quite scary and hard to explain to a child that we are actually in an elevator without a ceiling, so it just makes it seem as though the room is stretching. Vanessa wants out and spends most of the ride actually huddled into my arm or with her head buried in her hands.

Just when she thinks it's safe to open her eyes, a ghost appears, right in the middle of our carriage.

'I am never going on that ride again!' she says, still trembling.

'I thought it was cool!' Leon says.

'Yeah, me too,' Sam says.

It's nearing lunchtime, and the temperature soars into the nineties. We are buying bottles of water like it's going out of fashion.

'I'm going to take Vanessa for this appointment,' I say as we sit, drinking more water and deciding where to go next.

'We'll meet you there in about an hour,' Tom says.

We go off in the other direction, back to Sleeping Beauty's Castle and the Bibbidi Bobbidi Boutique.

Vanessa is having the Crown package which consists of hair style, shimmering make-up, and nails.

The Bibbidi Bobbidi Boutique is owned by the Fairy Godmother, and each girl is assigned a Fairy Godmother-in-training who performs the magic makeover.

The boutique is bustling with mums and daughters choosing princess outfits, hair accessories, and make-up. Beyond the store section is the reception desk, and then the boutique itself.

We check in and wait for our Fairy Godmother to come and collect us.

Margaret introduces herself as our Fairy Godmother. She leads us into the boutique and seats Vanessa in the chair, covering her with a pale blue cloak.

Vanessa chooses the Pop Princess style, which means tying up her hair and adding artificial hair, which spikes out in lots of different colours, with plaits tied at the ends with Mickey Mouse heads. Very cute!

Vanessa's hair touches her waist and so Margaret really has her work cut out for her, combing it all out, plaiting it, and tying it up on her head before fixing the coloured hair to it.

Mums are asked to sit on the benches, which run through the centre of the boutique. The girls face towards the benches, so they can't see themselves in the mirrors behind until the end when the Fairy Godmothers spin the chairs around and reveal their magical transformation.

Other Fairy Godmothers-in-training wander around, taking photographs which you can then purchase afterwards.

Kate and Shelby join us after an hour, just as Margaret is adding the finishing touches, doing Vanessa's nails and make-up.

'Are you ready?' I ask Vanessa as Margaret takes off the blue cloak.

'I think so,' Vanessa says shyly.

Shelby, Kate, and I have our cameras at the ready as Margaret spins the chair around.

'Wow!' Vanessa exclaims.

Her smile says it all.

'You look beautiful, honey,' Shelby says.

'Just like a princess!' Kate adds.

'A pop princess,' Vanessa says.

'And a beautiful one at that,' I say, giving her a hug. 'Happy birthday, sweetie.'

'Thank you, Mummy,' Vanessa says. 'It's so cool!'

We meet up with the others outside and decide we should get some lunch before going off to find Space Mountain®.

I'm not entirely sure what the ride involves, but it's in total darkness, and I already don't like the sound of it.

'You are going to go on it, aren't you?' Tom says.

'I would rather not,' I say hesitantly.

'No!' Kate cries. 'If I am going on it, then so are you,' she says.

'But after lunch,' I plead. 'Come on,' I say, trying to get myself out of it.

'Excuses, excuses. It's in the dark, so you won't be able to see anything, anyway,' Tom says.

'Like that is really going to make me feel better. That's worse!' I say.

And so, as promised, after lunch we make our way to Space Mountain.

You'd think the queue would put everyone off but sadly it doesn't. What bothers me most is that we seem to be pretty high up!

We finally reach the front and wait for the ride to come to a stop. Bars lift off everyone who has just been on the ride, and at that moment, I really want to run in the opposite direction but then think that if Vanessa and Leon can go on the ride, then surely I can too. Sam, on the other hand, isn't swayed by anything and has stayed with Shelby who, with a bad back, can't go on the ride even if she wants to.

I sit next to Kate, and she squeals with delight as the bars come down over us.

Tom prods my shoulder, 'You okay, Sis?' he says.

'Like you care,' I say jokingly.

Before I have a chance to say anything else, we jolt forward and are moving, and apart from stars, we are in total darkness. It's probably a good job really because I'm sure we are quite high up. The ride then goes so fast that I can feel the skin on my cheeks rippling.

Kate screams, 'G-Force!'

I put my head down and pray that I'll reach the end, letting out the occasional yelp when the ride takes a dive or makes an unexpected whipping turn.

Relief is an understatement in describing the feeling of coming to the end of the ride.

'Want to go again, Grace?' Tom asks.

'Oh yes, please, let's queue again,' I reply sarcastically.

'I hope you're happy now,' I say. 'I can't feel my legs. They have gone like jelly.'

Totally amused by the whole thing, Tom starts laughing.

'Come on, let's go look at the pictures,' Kate says, hurrying ahead.

'Pictures?' I say. 'You mean they took pictures of us, scared out of our wits, screaming our heads off?'

'Of course, they did,' Kate says.

We make our way towards the exit and to view the pictures.

Not surprisingly, I look crazed with my mouth wide open, screaming. My knuckles are white from gripping the bar in front of me like my life depends on it. Having said that, Kate doesn't look much better, and Tom looks like he's screaming like a girl too.

We stand laughing at ourselves until the people behind us ask if we were going to move on. We apologise for holding everyone up and make our way out to find Shelby and Sam.

The rest of the afternoon is spent revisiting the Haunted Mansion, Pirates of the Caribbean, and various other rides we come across along the way.

Antonio and Kate say they are going to head off for a couple of hours while we take the monorail to Toon Town. We arrange to meet up with them later for dinner.

By the time we catch the monorail back to Downtown Disney to meet Antonio and Kate, it's dark. We are all hungry and after so many hours in the sun, pretty worn out and tired too.

After dinner, Vanessa is desperate to have her portrait done in chalk by a guy who we saw earlier, and because this is quite close to the hotel, we agree I'll stay and do this with Vanessa while everyone else heads back.

It takes just under an hour for Mike to chalk Vanessa's portrait, largely because she has all this coloured spiky hair and plaits dangling, with little Mickey Mouse heads attached to them!

We arrive back at the hotel to find Leon fast asleep, horizontally across the bed.

'I'm not going to be far behind him,' I say to Shelby as we say goodnight.

Tom, whose favourite motto is 'I'll sleep when I'm dead' yells from the bathroom, 'Back to camping tomorrow.'

'Thanks for reminding us, honey,' Shelby says with a hint of sarcasm in her voice.

'Feels good to be going back to camping, I think', I say to Shelby, 'have kind of missed it.'

'You're as mad as he is,' she says, laughing.

'That was the best birthday ever. Thank you, Mummy,' Vanessa says, appearing in the doorway and giving me a hug. 'Thank you, Aunt Shelby,' she says, turning and hugging Shelby.

'Melts my heart,' Shelby says. 'If you could only meet Mr Right, then you would all move over here, and everything would be perfect.'

Sequoia National Park

Disneyland has been such a great experience, especially with it being our birthdays. Celebrating Vanessa's tenth birthday in Disneyland is something she will always remember, and we're very grateful to Shelby and Tom for making it all happen.

'Right! Come on then. Let's go people,' Tom shouts, banging on the door.

'We aren't packed up just yet,' I hear Shelby call after him.

Tom is eager to get back to camping and away from civilisation as quickly as possible.

It's 7.30 a.m., and we have all been up early with the intention of leaving by eight.

'I'm going to get some coffee before we leave, if that's permitted?' I say to Tom as I open the door to let him in.

'Only if you're quick,' he says, putting his hands on his hips sarcastically.

'Sometimes I think you would have been better in the army,' I say to him. 'All these years, I never knew you were this bossy!'

'Just want to get out of here and into the mountains,' he says. 'Which bags can I take?'

'We are packed but just leave the kids' rucksacks and my handbag,' I say, heading out the door.

Much to Tom's delight, we leave Disneyland a little after 8.00 a.m. Already the sun is up, ready to scorch the next 50,000 daily visitors to the park.

Our final destination is the Lodgepole campsite in the beautiful Sequoia National Park.

Our first stop, once in the park, however, is to visit General Sherman, the largest tree on earth. I love trees, and so this seems like the perfect place to end our camping trip.

The drive from Los Angeles takes us about four and a half hours.

As our elevation becomes higher and higher, Shelby begins to get sick. I don't think the twisty roads, with sheer drops help. As Tom tries to find somewhere to stop, I become increasingly worried that Shelby might have to pop her head out of the window and throw up. Obviously, being right behind her seat, I fear being caught in the backlash and urge Tom to hurry.

Past the next turn he finds a stop, and Shelby quickly gets out of the van and takes in some still fresh air. Tom jumps out to see how she is while I stay with the kids who are eager to see bears.

It reminds me of when we were little and used to go to the seaside, Great Yarmouth beach to be exact, and as we drew closer, would wonder who would see the sea first. In our case, it's who can see the first bear.

Shelby gets back in the van.

'You okay?' I ask.

'Yes, I think so. Just crept up on me but I feel fine now we've stopped,' she says, still looking a little pale.

'Maybe you should go slower, Tom,' I suggest.

'If I go any slower, I'll stop,' he replies.

We set off once again, and all hope that Shelby will make it to the tree trail without throwing up or at least, without throwing up in the van!

We reach the Sherman Tree Trail, and Shelby feels much better for feeling the ground beneath her feet and the fresh air again. The temperature, even at this elevation, is hot, but with so many trees for shade, it feels cooler.

The walk along the trail to General Sherman is about a mile downhill but obviously, that means uphill on the way back.

At the halfway point, we stop at a sign that informs us that at this point, we are half of the way up the General Sherman tree, in terms of how far we have just walked: 138 feet!

Named in 1879, after a Civil War general called William Sherman, its statistics are staggering. The tree is believed to be around 2,200 years old. It is not the tallest or widest tree on earth, but the overall volume of its trunk makes it the largest tree on earth. It stands at 275 feet high, and the circumference at ground level measures just over 102 feet! If the General Sherman's trunk was filled with water, it could provide water for 9,844 baths!

We all look tiny, standing in front of this enormous tree and of course, make the most of the opportunity by taking lots of photographs.

After leaving General Sherman, we drive further into Sequoia and finally reach Lodgepole campsite late afternoon. We are now at an elevation of around 6,700 feet and surrounded completely by forest.

We check in and locate our camp spot.

We all knew there would be bears in the forest, but the prospect of seeing one face to face hasn't seemed very real, until now.

Every campsite is assigned its own metal storage unit. On the front of each unit is a sticker warning that bears are active day and night and providing instructions to store all food immediately. There's a picture of a bear's head: like we wouldn't know a bear if we see one!

I can't believe that there's a very real possibility that a bear might just turn up in camp.

Shelby is concerned at the thought of being in the van on her own all night, but I feel we are more at risk in our flimsy five-man tent. At least Shelby is protected by all that metal.

A ranger comes by, and we flag her down to ask some more questions.

She instructs us that all food, and pretty much anything with a scent, has to be stored in the metal unit. That includes perfume, any toiletries, toothpaste, make-up, wipes, sun cream, lip balm, and so the list goes on.

The ranger explains that there haven't been any recent bear sightings in the campsite but that one of the campsites a little further down seems to be attracting them. She says people are being lapse and not putting food into their storage units, and provided we lock our food away in the storage unit at all times, we should be fine.

I joke that the bear will have an easy meal with five of us in the tent, but the ranger quickly assures me that bears are far more interested in vehicles. Rather too methodically, she explains that bears quite simply hook their claws into the top of the window and roll the side of the car down, a little like rolling open a tin can.

The colour drains from Shelby's face.

'Great! I'm now bear meat!' she exclaims.

Tom and I can't help but laugh.

The ranger assures us again that we'll be fine and goes on her way.

'It's not funny. You don't have to sleep in a van by yourself!' Shelby says, looking worried.

'Let's make sure we get everything into the storage unit now then, before the bear smells it,' Tom says.

'Are we going to get eaten by a bear?' Leon says.

'No, silly,' Tom says. 'Aunt Shelby is.'

'Tom!' Shelby shrieks.

'Oh, you know I'm only messing with you. You'll be fine. Like the ranger said, they haven't had any sightings, and this campsite is good because people are more careful,' he says, giving her a hug. 'Besides, I'm not going to sleep through tearing metal, am I?'

'Tom, that's not funny,' Shelby says.

'I know, and I'm just teasing. I can't help myself.'

We begin putting things into the storage unit. Everything seems to have a scent, and although we are probably being overzealous with what goes in, we figure it's better to be safe than sorry.

'Chewing gum!' Shelby yells, pulling out three packets from underneath Sam's seat. 'Are you trying to lure the bear in?' she says.

'Well, I didn't know that we would need to bear-proof the van, did I?' Sam says innocently.

I'm not sure how we manage to fit the contents of one van into a four-foot storage unit but we do.

We head off to the Lodgepole visitor centre to have a browse through the shop and get dinner.

It's a good five-minute walk away from the campsite, and we decide that we will not be coming back here after dark, at least not alone, anyway.

Our last night camping is spent around the fire, and yes, you guessed it, enjoying S'mores.

When we can't eat any more, Shelby informs us that there are still marshmallows, biscuits, and chocolate left over. We make a pact that we'll have them again the following night, by the outside fire at Shelby and Tom's house to toast the end of our camping trip. Any excuse really.

Despite all the hype, we don't encounter a bear visiting the camp in the middle of the night.

I get out of the tent early morning and find Tom crouching by a tree, taking photos of a deer that has wandered into our camp.

'I can't believe it's so close,' I whisper, the deer just a few feet in front of us.

'Obviously gets used to people,' Tom says.

I go back to the tent to fetch my camera and rejoin Tom to take some photographs.

'Well, you wouldn't get this close to a bear, would you?' I say to Tom as I inch a bit closer to the deer.

'Well, you might, before he ate you for breakfast,' Tom says, chuckling.

We are now just two feet away from the deer and obviously a little too close for comfort. As I take another photograph and the flash fires, the deer jumps up.

Shelby pops her head out of the van.

'Don't worry. It's not a bear, just Grace, scaring the deer,' Tom says.

'I'm glad to be alive,' Shelby says, smiling.

Tom laughs. 'It wasn't a bear you heard in the middle of the night, Shelby, just your imagination,' he says as he begins to make a fire.

Shelby relays that she was convinced that a bear had visited our camp during the night. She had a little too much to drink before bed and ended up waking up at 2.00 a.m., needing to use the toilet, in the worst sort of way. She says she was 'trapped' in the tin can and didn't dare to exit the van for fear of a bear attack. She tried to read to keep her mind busy, but that didn't work either. She ended up hearing all sorts of strange sounds that she had convinced herself were bears. She wrote in the journal we are keeping of the journey about how scared she was, and how each and every sound was freaking her out. Finally, when the sun started to rise and the birds started to chirp, she opened the van and shouted at Tom to escort her to the toilet. She ended up running full speed to make it in time.

We all sit around, with coffee and hot chocolate for our last morning camping.

'Well, this is it, homeward bound,' Tom says. 'It feels kind of sad to be going back to civilisation.'

'I can wash my trainers,' I say.

Shelby laughs. 'You have a real clean issue going on there, Grace.'

'I like my trainers grey,' Leon says, looking down at his feet.

'Me too,' Vanessa agrees.

'And I just buy grey ones!' Sam says, making everyone laugh.

We each take turns, saying which of all the campsites has been our favourite and agree that this one and Laguna Seca are tied first.

Tom the tour guide does his pack-man routine one last time.

We say goodbye to Lodgepole and the Sequoia Forest and head home.

Another Practice

I am pretty keen to return to San Francisco and practise yoga.

Vanessa and Leon are going to spend the evening with Mum and Dad, and then the following morning they are going to take them with Sam to the Kids Quest®, which is based in the casino close to where they live.

Since moving to California, the casino has become to them like bingo was when they lived in England, so frequented on regular occasions throughout the week.

Mum has always been lucky at the casino and regularly comes home with more than she goes in with. Dad, on the other hand, can spend hours in there and still come out with far less than he goes in with.

'So we'll be home after lunch tomorrow,' I say to Mum as she collects Vanessa and Leon.

'Have a great time,' Mum says. 'And don't worry about the kids. They'll love Kids Quest, and there's so much for them to do.'

Kids Quest requires parents to sign their children in and, under the strictest of security measures, leave them for a couple of hours to play while the parents then go and spend their hard-earned cash in the casino. The place is so much fun that, of course, the kids always want to stay longer, meaning that the parents just spend more!

'Enjoy the casino. Try to keep an eye on Dad, or he'll be selling the house!'

Mum laughs. 'I take everything off him before we go in: car keys, house keys, and importantly his wallet! We set ourselves a limit, and he goes off with that cash. Once it's gone, it's gone.'

'It reminds me of us when we were younger, going into the arcades and having so much money to spend.' I say, thinking back to Great Yarmouth beach and the arcades we used to spend hours in.

'That's exactly how it is. If he had his wallet, he would be withdrawing money like we have it growing on trees in the garden,' Mum says.

I laugh. 'Come on, guys!' I shouted up the stairs. 'Grab your bag on the way down.'

Vanessa and Leon race down the stairs and give me a hug.

'Bye, Mum,' they say together and disappear out the door before I have chance to reply.

Kate arrives shortly afterwards, and we set off for San Francisco.

We plan to stay in tonight, order a pizza, and play Scrabble®. Kate is the Scrabble Queen of California and is keen to add me to her list of conquests. Antonio said that he goes to sleep, dreaming about Scrabble because they play it so much. I haven't played since. I can't even remember and am not entirely sure I have actually ever even played Scrabble at all. English as a subject is however 'my thing', and I've always excelled at spelling and grammar and so am sure I can give Kate, who is highly competitive, a run for her money.

'So has Antonio ever beat you at Scrabble then?' I ask.

'Yes, several times, but I think every time there was far too much wine drinking going on, and so I always use that as an excuse for his victory,' Kate says.

I laugh. 'I'm sure he doesn't see it that way, though.'

'No, definitely not. He thinks he is slowly wearing me down and soon, using his words, the Scrabble tables will turn.'

We both giggle.

'You're making me nervous. I can't even remember playing Scrabble,' I say.

'But you're great at that kind of thing, so you'll be a good challenge,' Kate says, far too seriously.

'You make me laugh, Kate. You should find a Scrabble club and go compete.'

'I bet they are out there too, and you know what, I just might find one,' she says, even more seriously than before.

We seem to have a knack for missing the traffic, and once again, make our way over the Bay Bridge with little delay.

'That view never ceases to make me feel grateful for where I live, well, soon to live,' Kate says, looking over to the right.

The sun bounces off the glass windows of the tall buildings, creating a beautiful skyline as we headed towards San Francisco.

'I can totally see why you want to live here. It's beautiful.'

'You know, I never would have if it hadn't been for meeting Antonio,' Kate says. 'I mean I came to San Francisco often with girlfriends on nights out or with Mum and Dad, visiting, but it was always to the tourist spots, and San Francisco is such a great city when you go beyond that. There is so much to do and so many new things to see. I never get tired of being here, and I love it,' Kate says passionately.

'So you are going to stay, living here after you move in together, then?' I ask.

'Yes, definitely.'

'Sounds perfect,' I say, delighted that Kate is so happy.

'It is. I am so blessed, I have the perfect life,' Kate says, beaming.

We exit the freeway and make our way to Antonio's place.

'Are we ready for the San Francisco Scrabble challenge then, girls?' Antonio says as we walk through the hallway.

'Bring it on!' Kate shouts excitedly.

'Honestly, anyone would think you loved Scrabble,' I say jokingly.

Antonio makes us some tea, and I sit down to fuss Henry while Kate goes to find the pizza menus.

With pizzas on order, Kate sets up the Scrabble board while going through the rules.

'I didn't know there were so many rules to Scrabble,' I say, bewildered.

'There aren't!' Antonio replies. 'Kate has to make sure you know what you are doing and understand what is allowed and what isn't because if you slip up during play, you'll get an earful,' he says, squeezing Kate's knee playfully.

'And you should know,' Kate says. 'Antonio makes his own rules up and some of the most ridiculous words you ever heard of.'

'Just being creative,' Antonio says.

'We use the online Scrabble dictionary because then there is no question,' Kate says, switching the laptop on and positioning it at the side of the board.

'Ready?' she says, shaking the letter bag.

'I don't know!' I say, laughing. 'Scared more like.'

An hour later, having consumed most of the pizzas, I am in the lead. Not by much but still leading.

'I can't believe it. I've won!' I cry.

I jump up and start dancing, circling my arms around while chanting, 'I won, I won, I won!'

'Beginners luck!' Kate says. 'Let's play again.'

Antonio rolls his eyes. 'Now you see what I have to put up with,' he says and kisses Kate.

Had Kate not just won the second game, I think we would have spent the entire night playing Scrabble. Antonio manages to convince Kate that it's time for bed.

I need to be up early for yoga in the morning but can't sleep, thinking about seeing Michael again and putting a lid on this huge crush I have on him.

The next morning Kate drops me off and goes to have breakfast with Antonio.

'Hope you have a great practice, and we'll pick you up something delicious. Call me when you're done,' she says, waving as they drive off.

My legs feel like jelly, and I haven't even started my practice. I push the buzzer and wait for the door to open.

'Hi, Grace. It's great to see you. How is your trip going?' Michael says as I walk through the door.

Unfortunately, discovering that Michael is married and therefore strictly off limits hasn't made him appear any less drop-dead gorgeous than before. The sun coming through the window, dances on his sparkling blue eyes. They are just so inviting.

Oh my goodness! I'm standing here, staring at him. 'Get a grip!' I tell myself.

'Great, thanks, looking forward to practising again,' I say, wondering if he can read my mind.

'Oh no!' I exclaim. 'My mat, I left my mat in my sister's car! I can't believe that I've come here to practise yoga, and I leave the single most important thing in the car!' I say, feeling really cross with myself.

Michael laughs. 'Well, it could have been worse. You could have left yourself.'

'He thinks I am the most important thing!' I think to myself. 'He's married, and he didn't mean it that way. He's trying to make me feel better. Get a grip of your mad self, woman!'

'Do you have one I could borrow?' I say.

'You sign in, and I'll have a look. Generally not, but I am sure there are some that have been left and aren't used,' he says, wandering off into the other room.

He returns with a burgundy (of all colours) mat.

Burgundy is not a great colour for me. When I was eleven and Kate had just met her first husband (the Air Force pilot), we all went to Great Yarmouth to meet him. My mum insisted on me wearing this absolutely awful ensemble, which was made up of burgundy shorts and a burgundy striped vest top. I can still see it now.

I totally looked up to Kate, but the excitement of seeing her and meeting her new boyfriend was totally dampened by the fact that I was going to be wearing what looked like something that had been cut from a pair of polyester curtains.

My protests were a waste of time, and I remember spending the whole day, feeling angry at the awful outfit I was wearing. Of course, Kate had said how lovely I looked, but I know she was just saying that to make me feel better.

Ever since then, I've formed a great dislike for the colour burgundy and discovered much later in life that it doesn't suit my skin tone either. It makes me look washed out and ill looking. Shudder at the thought!

'Not a great colour, I know,' Michael says, interrupting my thoughts. 'But it's better than the floor,' he says, handing it to me and smiling.

'Thanks, Michael,' I say, grateful that he's found a mat I can use. 'I still can't believe I forgot my mat!'

'Don't worry about it,' he says, touching my arm kindly.

I think my knees will give way. Focus!

He continues. 'I once went to practise and forgot my shorts and had to practise in my underwear, although actually think these days it's more the norm,' he says, trying to make me feel better.

I try to hide my smile.

'Indeed,' I say, thinking about the practising Tarzan the last time I came to class.

I thank him again and walk through to the practice room.

Fortunately, the underwear-clad Tarzan isn't practising. I am one of the first to arrive, and after mumbling what I consider to be a half decent sounding chant of the opening prayer, I begin my practice, pushing all thoughts of Michael and Tarzan out of my mind.

Although I am grateful to Michael for finding me a mat, it isn't the best. Apart from the colour, it's also made of PVC, and so as I start to sweat the more, I begin to slip. My own mat is made of natural rubber and provides far more traction than most other yoga mats.

I also now understand what the Mysore mat I've bought recently is meant for. Because you sweat so much during Ashtanga yoga, even the stickiest of yoga mats still doesn't stop you from slipping. The Mysore mat is made from heavy cotton, and so by placing this on top of the yoga mat, it soaks up the sweat during practice, and because the cotton becomes wet, you don't slip.

Once upon a time, most yoga mats were made from PVC, which is not at all environmentally friendly and goes against the whole ethics behind yoga. If you are a true yogi, you generally live your life (as much as you can, anyway) in accordance with the yamas (ethical disciplines) and niyamas (self-observations). Ahimsa is the first of the yamas and basically translates to non-harming. Most yogis interpret this as non-harming towards themselves, others, and their environment, so it's easy to see that buying a PVC yoga mat just doesn't quite sit right (oh, these puns).

Fortunately, I have remembered my towel, so I place it under my feet, which provides enough traction to stop me slipping every time I go from upward to downward dog.

I am so engrossed in my practice that I forget all about the mat, Michael, and any other thoughts that keep clouding my mind. As I enter the finishing sequence, my awareness comes back to the other people in the room.

'Stand up,' Michael says, interrupting my thoughts once again.

I've just come out of the upward facing bow, which you'll probably remember practising when you were younger. I think we all used to call it the crab, where you put your hands by your head and lift yourself off the floor so you are doing a back bend.

'Stand with your feet apart and parallel,' he says, standing so close to me that I think we might Eskimo kiss.

He smiles, and his eyes light up.

'Just breathe,' he says, obviously sensing I feel uncomfortable, although I am sure not for the reasons he thinks. I wonder if he knows what effect he has on women. 'Focus!' I tell myself silently.

I smile back at him, doing as he instructs, letting out a long, slow, deep breath.

He places his hands on my hips. Does he really want to make me pass out?

'Inhale and take your hands into prayer,' he says.

I try to ignore the tingling running up my spine from his hands being on my hips and take a deep breath in, taking my hands to my chest in prayer.

'Now exhale and lift them up over your head as you fold back. When you see the floor, open out your arms and place your hands on the floor. Don't worry I've got you,' he says reassuringly.

I do as he says and can't quite believe that I've just done a back bend from standing.

'How in the hell am I going to get back up again!'

'Inhale and come up,' he says, pulling me up firmly towards him.

A smile beams across my face.

'Wow! I can't believe I've just done that,' I say, unable to contain my excitement.

He returns my smile.

'And again, inhale hands to prayer, exhale, and back,' he says, keeping a firm hold of my hips.

We repeat the posture twice more, and then I sit down on the floor, in a forward bend, with my legs extended out in front of me to counterpose the back bend.

Michael pushes his hands on my back to deepen the forward bend and my face sits neatly in between my shins.

This will have to go down as one of my best yoga moments: this and the wetting of the legs experience, of course.

I finish my practice and move into the relaxation room, glancing at my phone before lying down: 8.00 a.m.

I take some deep breaths and close my eyes, allowing my mind to drift rather than focusing on the incessant chatter that seems to waffle constantly through it for most of the day.

On an average, a person has around 64,000 thoughts a day. That's almost half a million thoughts a week! See, and there I go again, mind wandering off and thinking all sorts of weird and wonderful things.

After lying down for almost ten minutes, I call Kate quickly to let her know I've finished, roll up my mat, and go to say goodbye to Michael.

'Your practice is progressing well, Grace,' he says.

'I have learnt so much in just these few short lessons,' I gush. 'I'm so grateful to you.'

'You're welcome. Are you coming again?' Michael says.

'Yes, definitely. I am still amazed that I managed a back bend, standing up.'

'A lot of it has to do with your confidence to do it too, you know, and in time, you will be able to do it yourself without assistance.'

'Should I try it in my own practice?'

'Maybe not just yet, but we'll see by the time you go home.'

'Thanks, Michael,' I say, putting my palms together in prayer and bowing my head.

'See you soon,' he says and steps forward to hug me.

I resist the urge to throw my arms around his neck and instead, just hook one arm loosely around his shoulder to return the hug, pulling back so it doesn't seem I am lingering for too long.

I watch as he walks back to the class and then make my way out to reception.

A car horn sounds. I open the door and run out.

Kate and Antonio are both looking at me expectedly.

'Well?' they say together before I even had chance to close the car door.

'Awesome,' I say, relaying the back-bending experience.

'Here,' she says, handing me a breakfast pot filled with yoghurt and fresh fruit.

'Thanks, Kate, this looks delicious.'

'So apart from the back bend, how did the rest of your practice go?' Antonio says.

'Oh, you wouldn't believe what I did?' I say, telling them how I realised I had left my yoga mat in the car.

'That's hilarious,' Antonio says. 'You go off to practise and leave your mat,' he says and laughs.

'I know! Talk about distracted!' I say, my thoughts returning to Michael.

'Michael found me one to borrow, anyway, and the practice was just amazing. It gets better every time I go.' I say, explaining that I actually bent backwards from standing three times!

Lake Tahoe

Lake Tahoe is up there on my list of 'must dos' during this trip.

My parents paid for my younger sister, Anna, to have her wedding in Lake Tahoe. Unfortunately, I wasn't able to go, and, on subsequent visits, still haven't managed to visit. Kate and Antonio often spend weekends away there, and Mum and Dad are such regular casino visitors that they often receive free hotel stays there.

Despite there being fifty-eight casinos, gambling is illegal in the state of California. In 1987, the United States Supreme Court ruled that Native American Indian tribes could operate casinos outside state jurisdiction. Of the 109 tribes in California, fifty-seven operate casinos, all of which are on Indian Reservations, which is basically tribal land.

Gambling is, however, permitted in just over half of the states across America, Nevada being one of them. As soon as you cross over that stateline, the first thing you hit is a casino. Mum and Dad's kind of place!

As I mentioned earlier, Tom and Shelby's next move will be up towards Lake Tahoe, and so pretty much everyone has some close association with the place.

The closest I have ever come to visiting Lake Tahoe was during the Christmas 2007 trip, when we ventured into the mountains for a day out, sledging in the snow. We didn't have chains, so we couldn't drive all the way up to Lake Tahoe, but we drove to a point where we could see the lake. It was definitely a 'dangling carrots' situation, and so I was determined that on this trip, I will get my first experience.

With no plans for Friday, Tom asks whether there is anywhere in particular I want to go. I jump at the opportunity and immediately suggest we spend the day in Lake Tahoe.

Shelby will be out of town, investigating a case and is disappointed that she will miss coming. She suggests we organise another trip up before we go home. Like I am really going to mind that! I already know I am going to love the place. What could be more perfect, it has everything: sun, mountains, beaches, water, and trees. What makes it seem even more perfect is that during winter, it turns into a proper winter wonderland with a full season of snow! Lake Tahoe has it all.

Tom has been looking at the map and is sitting at his computer when I walk into the office.

'You all ready to leave?' he says.

'Just about. Have you decided where we're going?'

'Sand Harbor Beach, says here it's the best one in Tahoe.'

'Hard to imagine beaches by mountains,' I say.

'Tahoe is a pretty amazing place, and the beaches are like you are by the Caribbean Sea, clear emerald-blue water and white sand.'

'You really are taking this tour guide stuff seriously, aren't you?' I say, laughing.

'Come on, let's go. If it's as great as it sounds, it will fill up by lunch time. If we get there early, we'll have no trouble parking or getting a great spot,' he says, switching off the computer.

'I've packed some of the inflatables for the kids and the towels. You grab some snacks and water for the cooler, and I'll round up the troops,' Tom says.

We are soon passing through Placerville on Highway 50, heading towards Lake Tahoe.

'I'm back, back in the New York Groove,' Tom booms, singing along to Kiss.

Sam, Vanessa, and Leon sit along the back seat, nodding their heads to the music, looking like three nodding dogs you see on the parcel shelf of cars sometimes.

'Adding this to the playlist too,' I say, getting out my piece of paper, which I now keep inside the zip compartment of my bag.

We make a quick bathroom stop just outside South Lake Tahoe, still in California, and we're then soon on our way, heading for the North Shore and Sand Harbor beach.

As soon as we cross over the stateline into Nevada, the first thing we see is not, surprisingly, a casino, well, a whole strip of them actually.

'This is where Mum and Dad come, usually to that one just there,' he says, pointing at the MontBleu.

'Is this where Anna got married too?'

'Yes, Harvey's. We passed that first, back there, just across the stateline. It's quite busy here but as we head further round, it will be quieter, although I am sure the beach will fill up later.'

I am in total awe of Lake Tahoe, and as we head away from South Lake Tahoe, the views just get better and better.

Lake Tahoe is nestled at an elevation of 6,225 feet in the Sierra Nevada Mountains and was formed two million years ago. The lake as it is today was shaped by moving glaciers during the Ice Ages. It has some pretty impressive statistics too being twenty-two miles long, twelve miles wide, and a maximum of 1,645 feet deep. That's a lot of water!

I love trees and quote John Muir, an American naturalist and nineteenth century advocate of wilderness preservation, who once said, 'The coniferous forest of the Sierra are the grandest and most beautiful in the world . . .' For me, being surrounded by so many trees is like heaven on earth. As I said, the water, mountains, beaches, and climate just make Lake Tahoe spectacularly perfect in every sense of the word!

It takes me a while to get my head around the fact that we are no longer in California but Nevada. The stateline actually runs through the centre of the lake itself, and so half of Lake Tahoe is in Nevada and half in California.

Sand Harbor Beach is on the east shore, towards north shore Lake Tahoe, but not quite half way around. We pull into the parking area pretty early, about 9.30 a.m., and are pleased to see that there are only a few other people heading for the beach.

After having spent over a week, camping in the van, we are now pretty used to changing en route. Everyone jumps out while Vanessa changes into her bathing suit, and then when she's finished, Sam gets in and does the same. We each take as much stuff as we can carry, letting Tom take the fully inflated crocodile and the Yukon (the inflatable ring that is actually meant for the snow) and make the short walk to the beach. I turn around and laugh out loud, almost dropping my armful of towels and water bottles. Tom has the crocodile in front of his chest, and so it looks like his legs are some weird extension of its body.

'Keep walking, or you'll have to carry it all,' he says.

I laugh. 'A talking crocodile.'

Lake Tahoe is a freshwater lake, which has crystal-clear alpine water. Sand Harbor Beach has pure white sand, and if the mountains weren't in the background, I might think, just like Tom said, that we are somewhere in the Caribbean.

'How amazing is this!' I say excitedly as we head further along the beach.

The beach is quiet with just a few people dotted here and there.

'Let's take that spot just to the side of the lifeguard tower,' Tom says.

I turn around to see his head pop out from the side of the crocodile; he winks.

'She's got you doing it now!' I cry.

'I'm under orders. Shelby told me last night that just because she isn't here doesn't mean the hunt is off,' he says sternly.

'And here was me, thinking I was in for a quiet day of sunbathing,' I say, laughing.

'Just put your towels down, Grace, and do as you're told,' Tom says, throwing the inflatable crocodile at me.

Fortunately, the tower is closed up, and there are no lifeguards in sight. I hope they're taking the day off!

We set the towels down, and Sam, Vanessa, and Leon race down to the water's edge with the inflatables.

'It's freezing!' Vanessa squeals, running out of the water as quick as she went in it.

'It's an alpine lake', Tom says, 'which basically means a lake that's pretty high up and the water is colder. That's why it's so clear. You'll get used to it once you've been in a couple of times, and the temperature heats up a bit more out here.'

The temperature feels pretty good to me already, and I lie down on my towel to soak up the glorious sunshine.

'Don't look now but the lifeguards just arrived,' Tom says.

'I feel like an idiot already,' I say, opening one eye and peering to my right where Tom is now sitting.

I sit up and then lay back, propping myself up on my elbows.

'Why do you have your walking boots on? We're on sand for goodness sake,' I say, looking down at Tom's boots with his thick black socks rolled over the top. 'Why don't you ever wear flip-flops or sandals even?'

Tom roars with laughter.

'Yeah, right. Sandals are for Jesus and flip-flops are for girls. When we went to Hawaii for our honeymoon, Shelby tried to get me to buy some of those brown sandals, and I said that if she wanted Jesus, she was more than welcome to divorce me and marry him. I don't do sandals,' he says, shuddering at the thought.

'But you can get some nice flip-flops for men, and your feet would stay cool rather than being buried under those black socks and stuffed into those walking boots,' I say.

'Grace, have you seen my ankles and feet?' he says, untying his boot laces.

He takes his boots off, then his socks, and wiggles his toes.

I laugh at the perfect tan line above his ankle. His feet are at least four shades whiter than his legs.

'Apart from the fact that they look like they've been dipped in white emulsion, my ever-so-hairy legs stop being hairy in a perfect line too, making it look as though the hair is stuck on,' he says, looking down at his ankles.

I can't stop laughing. He has a point; even if his feet were tanned like his legs, the hair really does stop in a perfect line in the middle of his ankle.

'Do you shave them?' I say, trying to keep a straight face but unable to.

Tom throws one of his socks at my face and says that as he doesn't have any shoes on now, he is going in for a dip.

'You coming?' he says, heading down to the water's edge where Sam, Leon, and Vanessa are playing.

'I always worry what's swimming around my feet.'

'That's in the sea, Grace. This is Lake Tahoe and the water is so clear you can see the sand at the bottom.'

'You go. I'm going to catch some sun,' I say, lying back down again.

'Send out the vibe,' he says, nodding his head in the direction of the lifeguard tower.

I roll my eyes and ignore him.

It isn't long before the kids are talking about food, or in Vanessa's case hot dogs, and so we decide to go up to the restaurant, which is located a short walk across the parking area from the beach.

As we make our way over, we pass a bright green recycling station with the words ASS and PLASTIC, written in bold white letters across the top of the bin.

Tom laughs. 'Look, they even recycle ass up here,' he says.

I take out my camera; it is pretty funny to look at, someone having obviously removed the GL.

'What's ass?' Leon asks.

'Glass without the GL,' I say quickly, before anyone else can respond.

Sam and Vanessa giggle.

'Food then. Come on,' I say, ushering Leon towards the entrance of the restaurant.

The restaurant is more like a snack bar-cum-restaurant with a nice gift shop. We're surprised to find that it actually has a bar too. I don't drink, and Tom doesn't in the day, but it's far more sophisticated than we thought it would be. We can choose to take the food out or eat in and to the side, beyond the bar and shop, is a really nice walled patio area with views across the lake.

'Let's eat here,' I suggest.

Tom has fries, and I order a summer salad, which sounds delicious because it has strawberries in it. Vanessa, not surprisingly, orders a hot dog, and Sam and Leon decide that's a good choice and join her.

We sit outside, enjoying the views across the lake.

'I could totally live here. I love everything about it, and you could just not tire of that view,' I say, looking out across the lake.

The food is delicious, and after we've eaten, we look around the gift shop and buy a few postcards to send home, before walking back to the beach.

Sam, Vanessa, and Leon set about making sand castles.

'Why don't you go in the water, swim out a bit, and then splash around like you can't swim and shout for help,' Tom says. 'That way, one of those lifeguards will come, save you, and I'll have earned some brownie points with Shelby for the day.' He laughs.

'Right, and they'll wonder why you are sitting on your backside, not moving an inch to come and save me,' I say. 'Just take a photo of them, and we'll tell Shelby I spoke to that one there, with the dark hair.'

'She'll never believe you, not without a phone number as evidence,' Tom says. 'You forget she's a private investigator and nothing gets past her.'

'Just take the photo,' I say, handing him the camera.

'They might think I fancy them,' Tom says, looking quite perturbed.

I can't help but fall about laughing as he stands up and walks around being very effeminate while taking the photograph.

'You look like Ms Jay from that *American Top Model* show, doing his signature catwalk.'

He proceeds to do his best catwalk impression up and down the sand.

'You'll get a date if you keep that up,' I say.

'Shelby would be thrilled,' he says, laughing.

We pack up and leave the beach midafternoon.

'Do you think we'll get a chance to come back to Lake Tahoe?' I ask Tom as we drive out of the parking area.

'Don't see why not. I know Shelby really wanted to come, so we'll organise another day up here,' Tom says.

We decide to drive back to South Lake Tahoe by going all the way around the lake. The more I see, the more I like, and I decide that I like the north shore the most.

'We're back in California,' Tom says, pointing to the 'Welcome to California' sign as we pass through the stateline.

'Go back', I say, 'so I can take a photo.'

Tom turns around at the next lights, and we drive back just so I can take a photo of the sign. It seems so strange that one minute we are in Nevada and the next, in California. Somehow, I thought that one state would look so different from the next and that it would be very apparent when you went from one to the other. But it isn't like that at all.

We take in the scenic drive, and the views across Emerald Bay as we near South Lake Tahoe again are nothing short of spectacular.

'Can we stop on the way back for ice cream, Dad?' Sam asks.

Vanessa and Leon think that's a great idea, and Tom says he knows just the place.

We stop at Richardson's Ice Cream Parlour, on the drive out of South Lake Tahoe. As we pull up, there's a queue trailing out of the door.

'This place must be good,' I say to Tom as we park the van.

'It is,' Tom says. 'Every flavour under the sun, literally!'

We join the queue and decide what to order.

'Should I have a single scoop or a double?' I ask Tom.

'Grace, just look at that woman who just got her ice cream. That's a double scoop,' he says, pointing towards the counter.

Everything in America always seems twice as big as anything you ever get in England. Ice cream is obviously no exception. The double scoop is humongous and like a whole pot of ice cream lumped on to a big waffle cone.

'I think I'll have a single scoop,' I say.

We finally reach the counter and order.

We sit outside and agree we arrived just in time because the queue is now out of the door across the lawn and on to the pavement by the side of the road. All that for ice cream!

'I can't eat any more,' Sam says.

'Me neither,' Vanessa says, handing me her ice cream.

We all decide that as delicious as it is, there is no way we are going to finish it all.

We clean a very chocolate-faced Leon and jump back into the van.

I've thought that if I move to California, San Francisco will be the place I want to live. Driving back home, I decide that maybe Lake Tahoe will be a good place for me; it has it all.

Birthdays Barbeque

It's Mum's birthday and Shelby's, the day before we fly home. Due to the fact that Vanessa and I celebrated our birthdays while on the camping trip, Shelby decides to host a barbeque so that we can get everyone together and celebrate all the birthdays.

Shelby is the queen of barbequing, but she has to go out and run a work errand and so leaves Tom in charge. Her strict instructions are to watch the barbeque and turn it down (they have a gas barbeque) should the ribs start to burn.

Mum, Kate, and I are in the kitchen, chopping salad when Tom rushes into the kitchen, grabs a plate from the cupboard, and races back out again.

We down our tools and follow him out to the side of the house where the barbeque is.

Smoke is billowing out from the barbeque as Tom removes the ribs.

'Chargrilled,' Tom says, looking up. 'Shelby is going to kill me. Her strict instructions were to watch the ribs and turn it down if they started to burn!' he cries.

'They'll be fine with some barbeque sauce slapped on them, and besides, chargrilled is good, that's what barbequed food is meant to taste like,' Mum says, feeling sorry for Tom.

'We'll wait until they've cooled, taste them, and then I can always run out to the store and get more,' Tom says.

'It's meant to be good for your teeth, you know,' Mum says.

'What?' Kate and I say together.

'Charcoal, of course!'

'We'll relay that information to Shelby when she gets back then,' Tom says, peeling the last burnt rib from the grill. 'I can't see how anyone is going to want to eat these, and I don't think there is any meat left. It's all shrivelled up. I think I should get more.'

'Maybe that would be best,' Mum says, taking a closer look.

'We won't be long, and in the meantime, get rid of the evidence,' Tom says, handing me the plate.

'What if she comes back while you're gone and goes out to check the barbeque?' I say.

'I'm joking, Grace. Shelby won't mind so long as I run out and get more,' he says, turning off the barbeque.

Mum and Tom leave for the store, while Kate and I agree to finish the salad and then decide to start a game of Scrabble.

'You in for a game of Scrabble, Antonio?' Kate shouts over to the pool where Antonio is busy jumping in and out with the kids.

'What and get out the pool? No chance!' comes the reply.

We finish in the kitchen and set up Scrabble by the pool. Shelby arrives home shortly afterwards.

'Where's Tom?' she says, coming out to join us by the pool.

'Well, slight mishap with the barbeque,' Kate says.

'He burnt the ribs, didn't he, and now he's gone out for more,' she says.

'How did you guess?' Kate says, surprised.

'I know Tom. He and barbeques don't really mix, but I just keep leaving him in charge and hope that one day the penny drops, and he realises you actually have to check the food more than once every half an hour,' she says, starting to laugh.

'I'll go get us some drinks, and I'll join you for Scrabble. We've been playing nothing else since Grace got here, and I'm determined to beat her at some point before she goes home,' Shelby says, heading back towards the house.

Tom and Mum arrive back with more ribs, and Shelby puts them on the barbeque, relieving Tom of his duties.

Mum joins us for Scrabble by the pool, and the four of us sit under the shade of the big umbrella, while Tom and Antonio play in the pool with the kids. Dad snoozes in a lounger with his cowboy hat propped over his face to shade it from the sun.

'I'd put some sunscreen on if I were you,' Mum shouts over to him.

He doesn't reply.

'Maybe he's asleep,' Kate says.

'If he sits out in this heat for much longer without sunscreen on, he's going to be as chargrilled as those ribs,' Mum says, laughing.

'Dad!' I yell.

He jumps, and his hat slips off. He mumbles something and picks his hat up, putting it back on his face.

Dad has always been really funny when he's asleep, which is probably why he put the hat on his face. Usually his head will drop back and his mouth falls wide open. We have so many funny photos of him asleep, we could start a gallery. Then, if you dare to wake him up, he jumps, and his arms start flailing, or he shouts or mumbles something illegible.

Mum gets up and walks over to him. Sure enough, as she taps his shoulder, he jumps up again, arms flailing, hat flying, and mumbling.

He tells Mum in no uncertain terms that he has managed to last these many years without sunscreen, and he isn't about to start using it now. Besides, he tells her, he is getting a lovely tan. She tells him he is daft, leaves him to sizzle in the sun some more, and returns to the game.

Much to Kate's dismay, I win the Scrabble game.

'She's getting good at this,' Shelby says.

'Beginners luck,' Kate says.

We pack up the board, and Shelby goes to check on the ribs again. We decide we will organise the food inside, and then everyone can just help themselves and eat outside if they want to.

We leave Antonio and Tom in charge of the kids and go inside the house. Dad comes in shortly afterwards, positively glowing.

'Oh, Dad!' Kate cries. 'Go and look in the mirror,' she says, trying not to laugh.

'He's going to regret not putting sunscreen on,' Shelby says. 'If he's red now, imagine how he'll be later on when it really comes out more.'

Dad returns from the bathroom.

'Feels a bit sore,' he says. 'I don't know why, because I don't usually burn.'

'Well, you don't usually fall asleep in the midday sun,' Shelby says. 'There's some after-sun cream in the bathroom.'

The whole top half of his body is burnt to a crisp as though someone has just cooked him on one side. There are white lines across his torso where his skin has creased.

'I might go and put some after sun on then,' he says sheepishly.

'You should,' Mum says, shaking her head.

Dad goes off to soothe his skin while we get all the food sorted.

Antonio and Tom finally manage to get the kids out the pool and into towels, and we all sit around the table outside in the shade.

After eating, Tom and Kate disappear and return, each carrying a huge ice cream birthday cake.

'One for Vanessa and Grace and one for Mum and Shelby,' Kate says.

Everyone sings 'Hippy Bathday' because Tom has omitted the 'r' and rearranged the 'a' and 'i' candles.

Ice cream cake is the best birthday cake I have ever eaten and Vanessa, Leon, and I agree that we would like ice cream cake for every birthday, although we doubt you can get such a thing in England. They certainly don't sell them in grocery stores like they do in America! Now there's a thought for Sainsbury's!

Lake Tahoe Revisited

To continue celebrating the birthdays' weekend, we decide to head out to Lake Tahoe early Sunday morning, spend the day at the beach, and go for dinner somewhere on the way home.

After a 'spiderless' garage yoga session, I take a shower and round up Vanessa and Leon for some breakfast.

Tom is making his speciality pancakes and fashioning the batter into the letters of each of our names.

'Mine's L,' says Leon as he sits down at the table.

'I think he might know that,' Vanessa says, joining him and holding on fast to the maple syrup.

'It's not going to go anywhere, you know. There's plenty of syrup to go round,' I say to her.

Vanessa loves pancakes just about as much as she does hot dogs and simply insists on having the syrup first.

'We have another bottle,' Sam says, getting up to fetch the extra syrup from the pantry.

'Who wants the V?' Tom asks, bringing in the first plate.

'Me, me, I want it!' Leon cries.

'So, your name begins with the letter V, does it?' Tom says, raising his eyebrows at Leon.

Leon smiles cheekily, 'Well, no, but I'd like it, anyway,' he says hopefully.

'That would be me,' Vanessa says, licking her lips.

She pours a generous dollop of syrup onto her pancake and tucks in. Leon looks as though he might start drooling.

'You might want to do Leon next before he dribbles all over the table,' I say to Tom and begin making coffee.

Mum and Dad arrive shortly afterwards and join the table for breakfast. Shelby appears, and we all sit enjoying pancakes, toast, and coffee.

By 8.00 a.m. we're ready to leave. We plan to return to Sand Harbor Beach and get there before ten, ahead of the crowds, or at least before they close the parking lot, which they do once the number of cars exceeds their limit.

Leon decides he wants to ride with Mum and Dad in Mum's new PT Cruiser. We take the crisps and breakfast bars we find off him and say that he will have to eat when we arrive because he will no doubt fill Mum's brand new car with crumbs and strawberry jam filling.

We arrive at Sand Harbor Beach by 10.00 a.m., and although there's a trickle of cars into the beach, it isn't at all crowded, and we find a great spot.

Tom packed the chairs for Mum, Dad, and Shelby and looking at Mum reminds me of someone sitting on Skegness Beach on a freezing English spring morning. She is wearing jeans, black shoes, and a heavy fleece that she has zipped up to her neck and is huddled up with her arms folded.

'Mum, seriously, I am lying here in a bikini, the kids are in the water, and you are sitting here in this gorgeous sunshine, looking so wrapped up that I am afraid you are going to start melting!'

'I'm chilled to the bone. It was freezing this morning, and I haven't warmed up since,' she says, hugging her arms in closer to her body.

Dad strips off his T-shirt to reveal his stripy torso. I throw him the sunscreen.

'Better put this on today, Dad, although if I were you, I would put your shirt back on.'

Obviously feeling the immediate sting of the sun on his sunburn, he puts his T-shirt back on and begins liberally applying sunscreen to his legs, face, and arms.

'Well, I'm going to go in the water,' I say, standing up mentally preparing myself.

'I didn't go in last time we were here, and as you can see down to the sand at the bottom, I'll be able to see if anything swims around my feet,' I say, trying to convince myself I won't get eaten by a shark.

When I was a teenager, we moved to a house that had a swimming pool and for the few months before Dad decided to build an extension and make the pool derelict, we had a great summer in it. However, I can still remember swimming in it at night, scaring myself to death, thinking there were sharks around my feet. Sharks in a swimming pool!

'There are no sharks in Tahoe,' Tom says, reading my mind.

'Are you sure?'

'Grace, for a shark to get into Lake Tahoe, it would have to trek through some wilderness, and we both know that's not going to happen,' he says, laughing.

'Maybe someone put a couple in, they mated, and now you have sharks in the lake,' Dad says.

'Only you would think that, only you,' Mum says. 'Take no notice of him, Grace. There are no sharks in the water, just go in.'

'Come on, I'll come with you,' Tom says.

'What and get those pearly white feet of yours out of those boots again? Most definitely, come on!' I say, walking down to the water's edge.

Vanessa, Leon, and Sam are floating close to shore in the Yukon.

'Let's swim out to the buoys over there?' Tom says.

'No! Look how far away it is. It's miles out. I'm not sure that I'm that much of a strong swimmer these days,' I say worriedly.

'Sam, you can bring the Yukon out there, and then if Grace gets tired, she can jump in that,' Tom says.

'I'm not going out that far,' Sam says.

'I'll swim until the water comes up to my neck, standing on my tiptoes,' I say, 'and then you're on your own.'

We begin to swim, and although the water is indeed crystal clear, it's difficult to swim and look at what's beneath me at the same time.

'Grace, will you just stop trying to look down. There's nothing going to pop up and grab you,' Tom says, swimming ahead slightly.

'Don't leave me then!' I cry.

We swim further out and I feel okay. That is until I turn around to see that we are actually quite a long way out from the shore.

'I don't think I like this,' I say nervously.

'Just keep swimming. You'll be fine,' Tom says.

I stop swimming and bring my legs down, so I can feel the sand beneath the water, which is now lapping my shoulders.

'I might go back now,' I say, feeling too much out of my comfort zone.

'Come on!' Tom says impatiently.

'It's okay for you. You don't care about what's beneath you, but I do!'

'Just a bit further,' he says.

I carry on swimming.

Just then I feel something grab my ankle and tug. I scream, stop swimming, and my head goes under. I come up, my arms flailing, and splashing about in complete blind panic. I scream louder and hear roars of laughter as Dad appears from underneath the water.

'You are so mean!' I yell. 'And you!' I say to Tom, 'swim a bit further. Honestly, I'll never go in water again.'

Dad continues to laugh, 'We're only joking. It was so funny—your face! What a picture!' he says.

'I'm going back to dry land!' I say indignantly and leave the two of them treading water and still laughing.

'I told him not to do it,' Mum says when I come out of the water.

'It was like my worst nightmare come true. I'm surprised I didn't drown with all that screaming and splashing around.'

Vanessa, Sam, and Leon are playing on the sand and giggling.

'Ha ha!' I say and stick my tongue out at them playfully.

Mum finally decides to take off her shoes and changes into some shorts and a T-shirt.

Shelby is busy surveying the beach, no doubt for potential 'Mr Rights'. She never takes off her private investigator head, and I know what she is up to without even asking.

'Why don't you go do yoga over there?' Shelby suggests, looking in the direction of the lifeguard tower.

'Not on this beach. There are too many people and besides, how obvious can you get plonking yourself in front of a lifeguard tower doing downward dog!' I say.

Mum laughs.

'I never really understand why they call it downward and upward dog. I mean, it doesn't look anything like a dog, does it really?' she says.

Shelby and I fall about laughing.

'I would like to try some yoga, though. Maybe you can show me some.'

'I will, Mum, but not right here right now,' I say, much to Shelby's dismay.

'Just encouraging you to put yourself out there,' Shelby says.

'Yes, offering myself on a plate more like.'

'Or a mat,' Mum says, making us laugh again.

Dad and Tom swim back from the buoys, feeling quite pleased with themselves for having swam so far out.

'No sharks in sight,' Tom says, chuckling as he sits down on his towel.

'You'll get your comeuppance,' I say. 'Karma has a way of paying you back. What goes around comes around.'

'I am sure the universe will see the funny side of it too, Grace,' he says, starting to laugh again.

'Who's for hot dogs?' Dad shouts over to the kids.

Stupid question; Vanessa needs no persuading and comes racing back flicking sand all over my face as she plops down in the middle of everyone.

'I'd like a drink,' Leon says, thirsty as usual.

'You may as well just go drink the lake water,' Tom suggests.

'Don't tell him that, or he probably will,' I say.

'Won't hurt him. It's probably not that far off drinking water, anyway,' he says.

'Well, I'll take your word for it without him trying it,' I say. 'Come on, Leon, we'll buy you some lemonade.'

We bring lunch back to the beach and spend the afternoon, enjoying the sunshine and ignoring Dad's snoring. At least he has sunscreen on this time.

We end a perfect day in Lake Tahoe, driving back and having dinner at 'Islands', a tropical themed restaurant where, for Vanessa, hot dogs are definitely not on the menu!

San Francisco Zoo

With less than a week to go until we go home, I've planned one last visit to San Francisco.

We originally planned to go sooner, but I realised, fortunately before going, that it was a moon day and so the shala will be closed.

Practitioners of traditional Ashtanga yoga do not practise on new or full moon days, of which there are one of each a month, usually about two weeks apart. The explanation behind honouring this tradition is that water is affected by the phases of the moon, and our bodies, being made up of around 70 per cent water, are also affected.

There are nine moons, or lunar phases, and each depends on the moon's relative position to the sun. A new moon occurs when the sun and moon are aligned, and a full moon occurs when they are in opposition. Both the sun and moon create a strong gravitational pull on the earth.

In terms of yoga, the moon is said to vibrate different energy that can be likened to the breath: a full moon relating to the end of inhalation (when the pranic force is greater). This is energising, emotional, and uplifting energy, and a new moon relating to the end of exhalation (when apana is greater) which is a downward, slower, and more peaceful energy. These two lunar extremes can affect a yoga practice and create a higher risk of injury, and so it is therefore best to practise in-between these lunar cycles.

Observing moon days is also a way of respecting the rhythms of nature, and because Ashtanga yoga is such a physically demanding practice, it also allows for scheduled rest days.

We've now taken the drive to San Francisco so many times that I can probably drive myself. Shelby does offer her truck, but I decide that I'll feel more comfortable with Kate driving. As this is to be my last visit to San Francisco during this trip, I also decide to take Vanessa and Leon.

I'm due to go to class on Thursday, and so we head out late afternoon on Tuesday and are going to spend Wednesday at the San Francisco Zoo.

We take Vanessa and Leon on a trek around the area where Antonio lives, up the hill to see the Painted Ladies but spare them dinner at the vegan restaurant. Instead, we opt for pizza at a really nice and extremely busy restaurant across the street from Antonio's apartment. We place our order and are told to come back in thirty minutes when there will be a table ready.

We return, and the waitress seats us at the smallest table to seat five people ever, and Antonio quickly points out that there are actually five of us and not just two. The table is clearly meant for two people, and although Vanessa and Leon aren't adults, it's nigh on impossible for us to fit that many plates around the table. The waitress disappears and returns to suggest we all sit along the window bar at the front of the restaurant, as the people there will be leaving shortly. A couple are soon seated at our tiny table, and we move over to the window, which is kind of nice, anyway because it's away from the hustle and bustle of the main restaurant area, and we can watch the street go by.

Leon falls off his barstool, managing to somehow bang his head on the way down, which causes quite a scene as we try to detangle him from the stool legs while he screeches his head off, yelling 'me legs'.

'I knew it was a mistake, seating us at barstools,' Kate says, remembering her incident, falling off the barstool at the vegan restaurant.

Antonio laughs.

'Let's not relive that night, or we might get more than we bargained for on our pizzas. Anyone for oyster mushroom pizza?' he says in a devilish voice to Vanessa and Leon.

Leon half smiles between sniffles. His little red legs look sore where he's scraped them from falling off the stool.

'They'll be okay, pop,' I say to him, stroking his hair and leaning over to give him a hug.

'Careful Mum, or you'll be next,' Vanessa says, raising her eyebrow as I lean over to Leon.

The pizzas arrive, and we're delighted to see no mushrooms in sight. Antonio has chosen a meat pizza topped with jalapeno peppers and is daring Kate to eat a mouthful.

'You know I don't like spicy food,' Kate says.

'That's why I want you to eat one,' Antonio says, laughing.

As competitive as ever and never able to resist a dare, Kate agrees.

'Get the water ready,' Kate says, raring to go as Antonio stabs several peppers onto his fork.

'And you must chew and swallow them,' he instructs.

Vanessa and Leon look on excitedly; Leon now having forgotten all about his sore legs and more interested in Kate's challenge.

Antonio manages to slot six peppers onto the fork before cramming it into Kate's open mouth.

Her eyes bulge as she frantically chews the peppers, her arms swimming in mid-air as the heat begins to frazzle her tongue.

Leon giggles, and I grab his back to make sure he doesn't laugh himself right off the barstool again!

Vanessa picks up the water and hands it to Kate, who is now shaking her head and pursing her lips.

She swallows, reaches for the water, and gulps . . . and gulps.

Antonio is roaring with laughter and clapping his hands. Vanessa and Leon clap and cheer.

'That was awful,' Kate says after drinking the last of the water and pulling a face. 'My mouth is on fire, look.'

She opens her mouth and begins to scratch her tongue.

Leon and Vanessa laugh helplessly.

'I could do with ice cream before I eat my pizza,' Kate says.

'Yay!' cries Vanessa.

'No!' I say in the same tone as her 'yay'. 'Let's eat, and then we'll order some ice cream.'

We finish eating and ask for the dessert menu.

Vanessa and Leon opt for some sickly chocolate dessert drizzled in pure sugar, by the sounds of it, while Antonio and Kate order Spumoni.

'Spumoni, what's that?' I say.

The waitress explains that Spumoni is Italian ice cream made up of three different flavours, which are mixed with whipped cream with a layer of fruit and nut in between. That's all I need to hear and order it.

Kate, obviously following in Tom, the tour guide's footsteps, points out that there is actually a National Spumoni Day on August 21.

We decide to celebrate early; Spumoni is as delicious as it sounds.

We make our way back to Antonio's apartment, and Kate takes Vanessa and Leon with her to take Henry for a walk around the block.

I set up the Scrabble board ready for another late-night challenge while Antonio sorts out some movies he thinks Vanessa and Leon might like to watch.

Not surprisingly, Kate wins the Scrabble game hands down; well, two games actually. Vanessa and Leon have fallen asleep, watching a movie and as the last game finishes close to ten thirty, we call it a night.

The following morning, Vanessa and Leon are up, full of energy and raring to go. The excitement of spending the day at the zoo is too much for the apartment to contain, and so Antonio says he'll take them out with him to walk Henry while Kate and I get ready.

By 9.00 a.m., we are pulling into the parking lot of the San Francisco Zoo.

'Can we go and see the lions first?' Leon says eagerly.

'We'll get round to see everything,' I say. 'Let's just get inside first, find a map, and then we'll work out which way to go, okay?'

'I want to see the monkeys,' Vanessa says. 'Maybe we could adopt one?' she adds hopefully.

'What and take it home?' Leon says excitedly.

'No, silly, just adopt it. So Mum just pays for it, but it would be like ours, and we would get photos of it and stuff like that,' Vanessa says. 'Can we, Mum, please?'

'We're not even out the car yet, guys,' I say, trying not to commit to anything.

Antonio laughs as he gets out the car, scoops Leon up on his shoulders, and jogs off towards the entrance with Leon in fits of giggles as he jostles up and down.

San Francisco Zoo was originally Herbert Fleishhacker Zoo (the mere thought of a flesh hacking zoo owner!). It was established in 1929, and created in the 1930s and 1940s. At his suggestion, the name was changed to San Francisco Zoological Gardens in 1941.

The earliest zoo in San Francisco, however, dates back to the 1800s when during the Gold rush in 1856, the famous 'Grizzly Adams', who was actually James Capen, captured grizzly bears and kept them in a basement.

The zoo evolved when Robert Woodward, who amassed his fortune through the Gold Rush silver mining, opened Woodward's Gardens in 1866. The 'zoo' covered four acres and included bear grottos, an aviary, sea lion pond, and deer. The gardens were later closed in 1890.

The story of San Francisco Zoo began with a bear named Monarch, who interestingly was captured as a result of an assignment set by the famous William Randolph Hearst (remember Hearst Castle?).

You will recall that William Hearst was a media mogul, and at the time he owned the San Francisco Examiner. He got into a heated argument with one of his reporters, Allen Kelly, over whether grizzly bears still existed in California.

William Hearst wanted to present a healthy specimen to San Francisco to prove that the bears still existed and also to give the people such a fabulous gift!

Allen Kelly and a team subsequently went into the San Gabriel Mountains of Ventura County and, some nine months later, captured a giant grizzly bear which they named Monarch. The San Francisco Examiner was known as 'Monarch of the Dailies'.

William Hearst said that over 20,000 people came to Woodward's Gardens on 10 November 1889 to see the last and largest captive grizzly bear in California.

Monarch died in 1911 and didn't live where the San Francisco Zoo stands today. He survived over twenty years in captivity and was exhibited in the Natural History Museum, later being given to the California Academy of Sciences.

The sculptor, Robert Schmidt, who was tasked with designing the emblem for California, made a clay model of Monarch, which was later drawn, in 1953, and used as the bear design for the California state flag.

Vanessa and Leon charge through the entrance and race straight into the gift store.

'I thought gift stores happened at the end of the trip?' I say to Kate as we follow them in.

'I think they just position it right by the entrance so that you go in when you arrive and do the same when you leave, or at least, your kids go in so then you have no choice,' she says, laughing.

We find Vanessa and Leon in the midst of a huge pile of soft cuddly animals, all very cute and all working their charm on both of them.

'I can't decide whether to have this or this,' Vanessa says, holding out a baby monkey in one hand and a koala in the other.

'Who said we were getting soft toys?' I say.

'Antonio did. He said we could choose one,' Vanessa says, winking at Antonio.

'Well, who am I to argue then, but only one, guys,' I say sternly, knowing that they will try it on, and Antonio being as generous as he is will just buy them whatever they want.

'I'm going to have him,' Leon says, picking up lion.

Antonio takes Vanessa and Leon to buy their soft toys while Kate and I wander outside. The sun is already heating up and by the looks of things, we are in for a nice sunny day.

Each time I've visited San Francisco during this trip, the weather has always been warm and sunny, and we are really pleased that the day we decide to visit the zoo is no exception.

With Vanessa and Leon bounding ahead, we make our way along the path and into the zoo.

Our favourite, without doubt, is visiting the bears that are swimming around in the water in their enclosure. The lions and tigers are Leon's favourites, although they are all snoozing by the time we reach them. Vanessa says she likes the monkeys best, and it's hard to tempt her away from them, but we manage in the end, with the promise of a hot dog lunch.

The children's zoo includes a farm, which is home to pigs, goats, chickens, a miniature donkey, and sheep. The farm allows you to get up close to pet and feed some of its residents. We put money in the machine, which then gives us some food to feed the sheep and goats. They're obviously very hungry and begin huddling around us to get the food.

Kate starts hopping on the spot completely freaking out at the goats, huddled around her thighs, trying to take the food from her closed hands.

'Open your hands,' Antonio says. 'They can't eat the food while it's all balled up in your fists.'

'I know! But they're crowding me, I'm going to get trampled on,' she wails.

All I can do is laugh, and after a couple of minutes, we are all laughing so hysterically that we drop the food on the floor. The animals don't seem to mind; they eat the food and wander off to the next group of people buying pellets.

We make our way through the farm to brush goats. Yes, brush goats! Although I think the experience is far more soothing for the goat, I have to say. Every now and then, it has a quick nibble on my floaty top that keeps wafting in its face as I try to brush its coat.

'I need to get away from the goat. It's eating my top!' I cry.

'Better your top than you!' Kate says as we huddle together and made a mad dash out of the farm.

We wait for Antonio, Vanessa, and Leon, who are clearly enjoying the whole goat coat stroking experience.

One of the highlights for me, after lunch, is the Spider House. Of course, I am being totally sarcastic, and I don't want to go in at all, but Vanessa says if she goes, then I have little choice. After my experiences in the garage and during our camping trip, I feel I have seen enough spiders for one trip!

'Maybe it will be like the one on *Spider-Man* where the spider escapes and lands on your hand,' Leon says, dashing off to follow Antonio, who is peering into one of the cases.

'Maybe it won't,' I say to Kate, shuddering at the thought. 'It's making me feel really itchy, like there's one crawling around in my hair as we speak!' I cry.

'Oh don't, please, you're making me itch now,' Kate says, brushing the back of her neck.

'And me,' Vanessa says, shaking her T-shirt, just in case.

We walk around tentatively, peering in cases, but then backing off when we read the sign next to it that says it's 'deadly'.

'It's not going to get out,' Antonio says, standing beside Kate, tickling the back of her neck.

'Stop! You're making me itch more, and I already feel like one's creeping up my back as it is,' she says worriedly.

Leon giggles and rushes to see what's in the next case.

'B . . . R . . . O . . . W . . . N . . . R . . . E . . . curly C . . . L . . . U . . . SSSSS . . . E' he spells out carefully in phonics. 'What does that say then?'

'Brown Recluse,' Vanessa says.

We peer in to see the tiny brown spider in the corner of the glass case.

Antonio reads the sign, which explains that the Brown Recluse spider, sometimes known as the violin spider, because of its markings, has a venomous bite but is not usually aggressive.

'Well, I still wouldn't want to get bitten by it,' Kate says.

We all peer closer at the small brown spider.

I feel the goosebumps prick up on my arms.

'That's the spider! In Tom's garage, when I was practising yoga, it was just like that. Oh my god, I've been practising yoga with a brown recluse,' I cry, completely horrified.

'Are you sure?' Kate says.

'Yes, it was hanging from that Union Jack that was hanging on the garage door,' I say, backing away from the case.

'Well, maybe you should tell him that's what you think it was,' Kate says.

'I'm not sure I'll be practising yoga in the garage again before we leave.'

'As it says, they aren't aggressive, and it was probably just enjoying the yoga journey with you,' Antonio says, starting to laugh.

I laugh thinly, still hardly unable to believe that I've been practising yoga under the watchful eye of a venomous spider!

'What would it do to you? I mean, if it bit you?' I say, wondering whether that's a question I really need to know the answer to.

'I have no idea. It doesn't say on this sign. Let's ask someone,' Antonio says, eager to find out more.

'Do you really want to know?' Kate says.

'Yes, we do!' cries Leon, who is always up for a gory story.

Antonio locates one of the spider keepers who explains that although the brown recluse isn't considered a deadly spider, its bite can cause severe symptoms that include skin ulcers and lesions that damage the skin tissue, organ damage, and milder symptoms such as fever, rashes, sickness, and muscle and joint pain. He explains that very few deaths occur due to brown recluse spider bites, and those that have are usually in those with a weaker immune system.

'Nice!' I say, still reeling with shock convinced that it's the same as the spider in the garage. 'Can we please go now?' I say impatiently, wanting to get as far away from the brown recluse spider and his friends as possible.

'What a story to tell!' Kate says.

'Wow, Mum, you could have been eaten by a spider,' Leon says far too excitedly as we make a hasty exit from the Spider House.

'And that's one good reason for not asking the spider keeper more information about the brown recluse,' I say, laughing as Leon and Vanessa went to climb on the giant rope spider's web.

After petting some turtles and taking photographs of each of us with our heads sticking through boards with holes in them giving us various animal bodies, looking ridiculously funny, we make our way down the path and back to the point where just a couple of hours ago we began.

'The shop!' Vanessa cries.

They race off ahead before I can even open my mouth to speak, although disappear in the opposite direction when they see the sign for 'Adopt an Animal.'

'Well, that's gone and done it then,' Kate says.

Antonio laughs.

'Oh, come on. They won't be visiting San Francisco Zoo again for a while. Let them adopt an animal, and it's not like you have to take it home in your suitcase. Well, I don't think so, anyway,' he says humorously.

'They will be in there right now, telling someone which one they would like, so I don't see what choice I have, anyway!' I say and laugh as we headed towards the entrance.

Vanessa and Leon are busy at the counter, telling the lady at the desk why they want to adopt an animal.

We make a donation, and fortunately, the excitement of talking about adopting animals means that we can bypass going into the zoo store again!

One More Class

The next morning, I arrive at the yoga shala just after 6.00 a.m.

'Hi, Grace, how are you?' Michael says as he opens the door and smiles at me.

'Hi, Michael, good, thanks, although feeling a little sad as we go home next week. So this is the last time I'll be here this trip.'

'You're leaving already?' he says.

'We've been here now for almost six weeks. It's just gone so quickly. I'm really going to miss . . . '

The door buzzer interrupts my sentence.

'Sorry,' Michael says as he opens the door.

I was going to say I was really going to miss coming to the shala and being taught by him, but it doesn't seem appropriate now. The man who comes through the door sits down and begins taking his shoes off. Another couple come through the door.

'I think I'll go through and make a start,' I say to Michael, feeling slightly uncomfortable.

He nods and smiles.

I make my way down the hall to the practice room, set up my mat, mutter as much as I can remember from the opening prayer, still reminding myself firmly that I must learn it by heart, and begin my sun salutations.

Michael adjusts several of my postures, and I am delighted with myself at being able to roll back and up in the embryo posture without looking like a helpless ladybird and needing Michael to physically help me roll back up!

To this point, I've always practised the bridge posture, by lying flat on my back, bringing my knees to the sitting bones and then lifting my hips, rolling the shoulders underneath, and clasping the hands together. In Ashtanga yoga, however, this posture is practised by rolling the head back so that, apart from the feet which are spread open from the heels, the whole body is lifted off the ground. The hands are then crossed over the chest. I think the fear of snapping my neck has always prevented me from attempting this posture in its full essence previously, but Michael assures me, much to my embarrassment, that if I clench my buttocks (why do Americans always use that word like they are saying butter clocks!), the weight will not all fall on the top of my head. I hope he won't check whether my 'butter clocks' are clenched as I proceed to roll back on to my head and lift my body up.

I can't believe I've finally achieved this posture, but I can't smile for fear of unclenching my bum as I do so! It's a bit like trying to tap your head and rub your tummy at the same time; if my bum smiles, I'll fall down and probably really hurt my neck in the process!

I enter the finishing sequence and stand up to wait for Michael to take me into the back bends. It makes me feel so nervous: him standing so close to me and no matter how much I try to tell myself that he is my teacher and need to respect that I can't stop my breathing, becoming completely out of control and my heart feeling like it's going to jump right out of my mouth.

'You okay?' Michael says as he stands in front of me with his hands on my hips.

'Of course, I'm not okay,' I think to myself. If you leaned forward an inch your lips would be practically brushing mine! What a stupid question!

'Yes, I'm fine,' I say, lying completely.

I close my eyes for a brief second as I bring my hands to prayer, then open them, smile at him, and inhale up and over, which is where I want to be because if I stand that close to him for another second, I think I might kiss him.

He pulls me back up and as our eyes meet, I feel as though time stops still. One of those surreal *Mills and Boon* moments . . . '*he grabs her, forcefully pulling her towards him. Powerless to his magnetic charms, she melts into his chest, and he kisses her lips, tenderly at first . . .*'

Oh, for the love of God, I need to get a grip!

'Just need to catch my breath,' I say, trying to stop myself from completely losing the plot.

'Okay, just take as much time as you need,' he says, still looking into my eyes.

I inhale again and bend backwards, deepening the back bend by bringing my hands closer to my feet. My body feels so supple and flexible, and I am sure the sudden surge of heat has nothing to do with yoga but more to do with my thoughts about Michael.

I come back up again.

'One more time?' he says.

'Okay,' I say, inhaling immediately and bending backwards again.

I rest in a forward bend and finish the sequence before rolling up my mat to go into the relaxation room. As I was the first to practise, I am relieved to find the room empty.

Relaxing and sitting still isn't something I find easy, and at times, I literally have to force myself to remain on the mat, relaxing for just a little bit longer. I think, this time, however, I don't really want to leave. I breathe out a huge sigh and feel my back sink into the floor beneath me. Tears suddenly fill the corners of my eyes and spill on to my cheeks. I can't believe how emotional I feel; perhaps a combination of the trip being almost over and having to leave California, the place I love so much, and today, marking the end of my time, practising here.

I wipe the tears from my face and sit up, giving myself a few minutes focusing on my breath. I roll my mat up and am just standing when Michael comes to the top of the steps.

'You've done so well, Grace, I hope you've enjoyed your time here,' he says.

I feel the tears sting my eyes again but am determined not to cry in front of him. Then he will think I'm mad.

He leans forward and hugs me. I fight back the tears and hug him back. Despite the fact that I do still have a huge crush on him, I am overcome with gratitude for him, teaching me so much in such a short space of time.

He places his hands together and bows his head, 'Namasté', he says. Namasté is a Sanskrit greeting, which basically means honouring the divine present within you that is also present within me.

With my hands together in prayer, I return the gesture, bow my head to him, then look up, and smile.

'Bye, Michael,' I say, feeling peaceful as I turn to leave.

I walk back through the entrance room with tears streaming down my face. Fortunately the room is empty, so I sit down to ring Kate.

'It's me,' I say, sounding something like a wailing Chinaman.

'What's wrong?'

'Oh, you know, the end of the trip, goodbyes, last yoga class, and all that,' I say, sniffing and trying to stop myself from having a full-on meltdown.

Goodbyes are something we have all gotten used to. When I was seven, I came home from school one day, and my three brothers and sister had gone to Suffolk to live with one of the other mothers (also explaining further how Kate came to meet her first husband). Although I understand some of the dynamics of it all, I didn't then, and there was just Tom and I left at home (the younger brother and sister we have came afterwards). So, goodbyes to my brothers and sisters always feel harder, especially Tom, because with three siblings having left, I stuck fast to him like my life depended on it.

At least once a year, one of us will visit California or vice versa, and so the goodbyes are inevitable. Sometimes if another trip is planned, the wailing is probably less, but this time probably not so much because it has been such a fantastic trip, and I really don't want to leave now more than ever.

'I know how it is, but you'll be back. It's okay. I'll be there in a few minutes,' Kate says, trying to make me feel better.

'I'm okay, just came out of nowhere. I'll see you in a minute.'

Kate arrives shortly afterwards, and we take a few last photographs of me outside the yoga shala. I get in the car and look over at the yellow door and smile. It really has been a great experience practising here and something that I should feel happy about, not sad.

'You okay?' Kate says.

'Awesome,' I say.

Long Way Down the Holiday Road

Tom doesn't have the nickname of 'pack man' for nothing. His ability to pack the impossible is nothing short of miraculous. With great confidence, I hand him our remaining two big bags, (the third is still in the garage, having been put there when we arrived, following an in-flight gravy granule explosion) and neatly pile everything in great big mounds around the bedroom floor.

I can't believe we've accumulated so much stuff. The birthday presents obviously add to the volume, but there just seems so much more than when we got here.

Tom appears in the doorway and raises his eyebrows 'travelling light then I see.'

'I don't know where it's all come from. We didn't have this much when we came, and I have no idea how you are going to get it in three bags. I just trust you will,' I say, patting his shoulder and leaving the room.

Sure enough, he manages to somehow squash the impossible into three bags, and we are all set.

Because our plane leaves tomorrow afternoon from San Francisco, and Tom and Shelby will be working, we decide that it will work better all round to stay at Antonio's place tonight. It was poor planning on my part that we are leaving on the night of Shelby's birthday. When I booked our flight, I thought it would be fine because it's the 11th, the day after Shelby's birthday, although didn't give all the logistics much thought. Still Shelby being Shelby takes it all in her stride and says that it would be lovely if we all went to dinner to celebrate her birthday together before we leave. We agree on the Old Spaghetti Factory, and with our luggage now crammed into Kate's car, we will be leaving for San Francisco after dinner.

I take one last walk up to the pool before we leave, picking up the book I finished earlier still on the sun lounger. I look out up the hill beyond the garden and take a deep breath, drinking in the sunshine and the views from the pool one last time. Tom joins me, and I hand him the book.

'That has to be one of the funniest books I've ever read.'

'It is pretty funny and made me laugh out loud a lot of the way through.'

'Me too. It was hilarious, and I can't believe some of the facts he came out with. I never even realised half of that stuff.'

Tom loaned me his copy of Bill Bryson's *A Walk in the Woods*: a travel memoir of his trek along the famous Appalachian Trail, which runs in eastern America from Georgia to Maine.

'Reading that book got me thinking: I could write a book about our trip this year.'

'You've always wanted to write a book, Grace, you should,' Tom says encouragingly.

'I might just do that,' I say, thinking about what I might call it.

Dinner is nice but somewhat marred by the fact that we know the goodbyes are coming.

We congregate around the cars. In turn, we begin to say our goodbyes, and as expected, everyone is in tears—I, more than anyone else!

Antonio and Kate are in the early stages of planning a trip round Europe in autumn, so we'll be getting together for a week then. Mum and Dad are also planning on coming over to England for Christmas. Tom likes to visit England once a year, and Shelby says she'll come too. It doesn't make it easier, though.

'We'll be over next year, and you can come again next summer,' Tom says.

I puff out my breath between sobs and nod my head. 'I know, I know, it's just these goodbyes,' I say, giving him one last hug.

We get into Kate's car as Mum and Dad drive out of the parking lot. Tom, Shelby, and Sam get into their car and follow. We all wave and shout goodbye from the windows as they disappear around the corner.

I settle back into the seat and close my eyes, trying to stop the tears falling down my face. I wonder if I'll ever end up in California.

As we near San Francisco, the sun begins to set on the bay and to the right is the most magnificent sunset I think I have ever seen. The whole sky is dark orange and deep red as the sun appears to dip into the water. Sunsets and sunrises are among my favourite things to photograph, and I make the most of the opportunity.

We get to Antonio's apartment, and, after such an emotional evening, decide to call it a night ready for our early departure in the morning.

'Here we are again,' Kate says as we stop at the entrance to departures.

Although we'll be seeing each other in a couple of months, it doesn't stop us both from crying as we hug and say our final goodbyes.

'Wey, hey, hey,' Antonio says to Leon and winks as he scoops him up and gives him a hug.

'Wey, hey, hey,' Leon says, winking back at Antonio.

We walk through and keep turning to wave.

Tears stream down my face as we make our way through security.

'It'll be okay, Mummy,' Leon says, stroking my hand.

'I know. I just miss everyone,' I say, squeezing his hand.

'But we've had a good time,' Vanessa says.

'Yes, we have, an awesome time.'

Our plane leaves on time, and as we taxi down the runway, ready for take off, I close my eyes and focus on my breathing. We take off, and I open my eyes as the plane banks round. I can see the bay beneath us and the sun sparkling on the water below.

I look across at Vanessa and Leon and smile at them, madly pushing the buttons, trying to get their TVs to work. They totally live in the moment; perhaps I should take a leaf out of their book.

I close my eyes again and think about how I'd thought that the holiday road would lead me to meeting 'Mr Right' and ending up living happily ever after in California, drifting off into some Pacific Ocean sunset. He's still out there somewhere, 'Mr Right', I mean, but it feels as though my vice-like grip on finding him has lessened, and I trust that when the time's right, he'll appear.

Just like yoga, the holiday road became more about the journey than achieving an end result: spending quality time with my family, having a good time, visiting and experiencing some awesome places along the way, and realising that life is really about enjoying the journey.

Namasté!

Practise and all is coming!
Sri K. Pattabhi Jois

Ashtanga Yoga

Opening and Closing Sanskrit Prayers

OM
vande gurunam caranaravinde sandarsita svatma sukhava bodhe
nih sreyase jangalikayamane samsara halahala mohasantyai

abahu purusakaram sankhacakrasi dharinam
sahasra sirasam svetam pranamami patanjalim

I bow to the lotus feet of the gurus
The awakening of ones own self revealed,
Beyond better, acting like the jungle physician,
Pacifying delusion, the poison of samsara

Taking the form of a man to the shoulders
Holding a conch, a discus and a sword,
One thousand heads white,
To Patanjali, I salute.

Svastiprajabhyah paripalayantam nyayena margena mahim mahisah gobrahmanebhyah subhamastu nityam lokasamasta sukhinobhavantu
OM

May all be well with mankind
May the leaders of the earth protect in every way by keeping to the right path,

May there be goodness for those who know the earth to be sacred,
May all the worlds be happy!

Ashtanga Yoga

In addition to the five rounds of each of the sun salutations (Surya Namaskara A and B) in the primary series (Yoga Chikitsa) of Ashtanga yoga, I practise fifty-eight postures, and this includes those which have three or four variations.

Kino MacGregor, who is one of a select group of people to receive the certification to teach Ashtanga yoga by its founder Sri K. Pattabhi Jois in Mysore, India, is the youngest woman to hold this title. She has completed the challenging third series and is now learning the fourth series. Visit *www.kinoyoga.com* and *www.miamilifecenter.com*

Kino kindly shared photographs of each of the postures I focus on in the book.

Garbha Pindasana (Womb Embryo Posture)

Upavistha Konasana

Setu Bandhasana

Urdhva Dhanurasana

Sirsasana B (Head Standing B Posture)

Holiday Road
Playlist

Holiday Road—Lindsey Buckingham
Mr Wendell—Arrested Development
Cruel Summer—Bananarama
Dancin' with Myself—Billy Idol
The Tide is High—Blondie
We All Need a Little Shelter—Cinderella
Sweet Toxic Love—Culture Club
Armagedden It—Def Leppard
Everything—Depeche Mode
Hungry Like a Wolf—Duran Duran
Olivers Army—Elvis Costello
Thorn in My Side—Eurythmics
A Good Heart—Feargal Sharkey
I Don't Wanna Dance—Eddy Grant
Pour Some Sugar on Me—Def Leppard
November Rain—Guns and Roses (I know very random!)
Town Called Malice—The Jam
Crash—The Primitives
Cotton Eye Joe—Red Necks
Baby I Love You—The Ramones
Nessun Dorma—Pavarotti
Love Rescue Me—U2
I Wish It Would Rain—Phil Collins (and we wondered why it rained that day!)
They Will Be Done—Martika
The Ghost of Tom Joad—Bruce Springsteen
Back in the New York Groove—Kiss

Purple Rain—Prince (we so willed that rain to come!)
Stay—Shakespeare's Sister
Kokomo—The Beach Boys
Thank You—Dido

Lightning Source UK Ltd.
Milton Keynes UK
26 March 2011

169932UK00001B/34/P